CRITICAL PUBLISHING

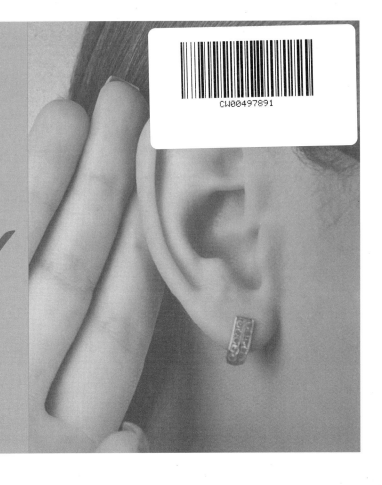

# Mentoring

Getting it right ✔

# IN A WEEK

Jonathan Gravells

Series editor: **Susan Wallace**

First published in 2017 by Critical Publishing Ltd

British Library Cataloguing in Publication Data

A CIP record for this book is available from the British Library

ISBN: 978-1-911106-28-9

This book is also available in the following e-book format:
MOBI: 978-1-911106-29-6

The right of Jonathan Gravells to be identified as the Author of this work has been asserted by him in accordance with the Copyright, Design and Patents Act 1988.

Cover and text design by Out of House Limited
Project Management by Out of House Publishing Solutions

Typeset by Out of House Publishing Solutions
Printed and bound in Great Britain by TJ International, Padstow

Critical Publishing
3 Connaught Road
St Albans
AL3 5RX

www.criticalpublishing.com

For orders and details of our bulk discounts please go to our website www.criticalpublishing.com or contact our distributor NBN International by telephoning 01752 202301 or emailing orders@nbninternational.com.

MIX
Paper from responsible sources
FSC
www.fsc.org   FSC® C013056

# CONTENTS

## Meet the author

### Jonathan Gravells

*I am a consultant specialising in mentoring and coaching, and over the last 13 years or so I have had the opportunity to work extensively in the education sector, as well as with multi-national companies, the National Health Service and small charities. In addition to being a practising mentor and coach myself, I have spent much of my time running training courses for mentors and coaches in schools, colleges and universities. I live near Lichfield in Staffordshire and, when not working or writing, I divide my time between cycling, family history and preventing a large garden from reverting entirely to natural wilderness!*

*I can be contacted at jonathan@fargoassociates.com.*

## Meet the series editor

### Susan Wallace

*I am Emeritus Professor of Education at Nottingham Trent University where part of my role has been to support trainee teachers on initial and in-service teacher training courses. My own experience of classroom teaching has been mainly with 14 to 19 year olds, and I have also worked in a local authority advisory role for this age group. My particular interest is in the motivation and behaviour management of reluctant and disengaged learners, and I've written a number of books and research papers on this topic. My work allows me the privilege of meeting, observing and listening to teachers from all sectors of education. It is to them that I owe many of the tips and ideas contained in this series.*

# Introduction

Welcome to ***Mentoring: Getting it Right in a Week***! Over the course of the next seven days you will learn all you need to know to be an effective mentor to your colleagues and to ensure that mentoring in your school or college is implemented, evaluated and embedded in a professional and sustainable way.

This book is aimed squarely at the busy classroom teacher, providing practical advice and helpful strategies in accessible, bite-sized chunks that are brief and to the point, and illustrated with clear examples, showing how you can put your new-found skills and knowledge into practice day by day. If you are already mentoring someone, then you may find it easier to spread reading these chapters over a longer time, even several months, in order to fit in with the frequency of your mentoring sessions. This will give you time to put some of the techniques and strategies into practice. But, however you choose to engage with the book, the chapters are designed to enable you to assimilate the important concepts and practices of mentoring in an easily digested and entertaining way.

Whether you are a new or experienced teacher, working in primary, secondary or further education, you will find this book both an engaging first introduction to mentoring and a useful opportunity to refresh and maybe extend your knowledge. Can you really become a great mentor in a week? Well, it's fair to say that great mentors, like great teachers, never stop learning and improving. But we certainly hope that, by the time you finish this book, you will be a more skilful and confident mentor than when you started.

Furthermore, because we know that great teachers are often given the 'career development opportunity' of actually implementing mentoring in their school, this book will not only introduce you to the skills and techniques you will need to be a good mentor, but will also enable you to impress your leadership team with your knowledge of how the school as a whole can ensure it gets the most from this important development process. (In fact, your head teacher may also benefit from reading this book!)

Over recent years, mentoring has attracted more and more attention as a critical element in the professional development of teachers, featuring in Ofsted reports, and taking a higher profile in schools' strategic plans for raising performance and quality of teaching. In 2008, a research team from the University of Nottingham and Leeds' schools of education conducted a literature review of the available research from around the world on mentoring new teachers. They concluded that mentoring could result in a wide range of benefits for individual teachers and schools, including:

* **For those being mentored**
    * reduced feelings of isolation;
    * adaptation to expectations and norms of institution/profession;
    * increased confidence and self-esteem;
    * professional growth;
    * improved behaviour and classroom management skills;
    * improved time management;
    * improved self-reflection and problem-solving capacities;
    * gaining perspective on difficult experiences;
    * increasing morale and job satisfaction.

- For the mentors themselves
  - positive impact on personal and professional development;
  - improved ability to learn and reflect on own practice;
  - opportunity to talk to others about teaching and learning;
  - new and improved teaching styles;
  - improved communication skills;
  - satisfaction and pride in helping others succeed;
  - enhanced career planning by identifying own priorities.
- For the school as a whole
  - increased retention and stability;
  - staff getting to know each other better;
  - increased collaboration;
  - more developed culture of professional development;
  - more cost-effective training and development of staff.

(Hobson et al, 2009)

In May 2014, Sir Andrew Carter was appointed to chair an independent review into initial teacher training. One of the specific remits of this review was to look at what elements create really effective mentoring. In his review, Sir Andrew called for a set of non-statutory standards *'to help bring greater coherence and consistency to the school-based mentoring arrangements for trainee teachers'*. The Teaching Schools Council invited a group of practising school leaders to help carry out this piece of work and consulted with a range of mentors, mentees and those responsible for managing initial teacher training in schools. They reported back in July

2016 with a set of national standards, and this document is now available on the gov.uk website (www.gov.uk/government/uploads/system/uploads/attachment_data/file/536891/Mentor_standards_report_Final.pdf).

It describes mentor standards in four distinct but interconnected areas:

- personal qualities;
- teaching;
- professionalism;
- self-development.

The stated purpose of these standards is threefold:

1. To foster greater consistency in the practice of mentors by identifying the effective characteristics of mentoring.
2. To raise the profile of mentoring and provide a framework for the professional development of current and aspiring mentors.
3. To contribute towards the building of a culture of coaching and mentoring in schools.

Many of the key findings and recommendations of this report are echoed in the chapters that follow. Furthermore, because the report promotes the use of mentoring beyond initial teacher training, the guidance and the strategies in this book are deliberately aimed at *all* mentors, whether working with trainee teachers, NQTs or more experienced colleagues.

The book begins by looking at exactly what mentoring is and how it works.

On **Day 1** you will learn about the role of the mentor, how to structure productive mentoring conversations and how you can help your mentee to do their best thinking. As outlined in the standards, it emphasises the need for mentors to provide appropriate support and challenge as well as signposting other sources of expertise and knowledge. Equally importantly, you will learn to distinguish between your role and responsibilities as a mentor and those responsibilities that you should leave firmly with your mentee.

On **Day 2** the focus is on how to make mentoring work well in your school, touching on key recommendations from the standards, such as a systematic process for identifying and training mentors, and the importance of providing continuing mentor development. Day 2 will also help you to identify what you want the mentoring to achieve and how to get and maintain colleagues' commitment to the process. Importantly, you will learn more about the negative consequences of getting mentoring wrong.

On **Day 3** you will learn about the importance of building the right quality of relationship with your mentee. Establishing trusting relationships and empathising with a mentee's challenges form part of *'personal qualities'*, the first of the four standards specified in the TSC report. You will be introduced to strategies for ensuring a 'safe space' for your mentoring conversations and the necessary ground rules for making this work. Finally, you will discover how to locate the boundary between being a supportive mentor and being a sympathetic colleague or friend.

**Days 4 and 5** focus on the specific skills you will need to develop in order to be a great mentor. As recommended in the national standards, these include a range of interpersonal skills, such as listening, questioning as well as summarising and reflecting back and using shifts in perspective to re-frame challenges and blockages to development. The standards rightly emphasise the importance of mentors being able to provide effective feedback, and so you will learn more about the different ways a mentor can apply this crucial skill.

On **Day 6** you will find out more about how these skills and techniques can be combined to enable you to address some of the common challenges that all mentors encounter at some time. These include:

- raising your mentee's self-awareness;
- helping your mentee develop productive relationships with colleagues, students and parents;
- building resilience in your mentee;
- supporting your mentee to achieve sustainable behaviour change.

The national standards also emphasise the importance of mentors continuing to develop their practice, and so on **Day 7** you will be given strategies for evaluating your practice and the effectiveness of the mentoring, with a view to improving the quality of mentoring at both an individual and school level.

In order to help you navigate all of this easily, each chapter (or Day) follows the same format, comprising a number of interlocking elements.

**Chapter opener:** The day's topic is introduced and put in context with a brief explanation of why it is important and how it links to other subjects covered elsewhere in the book.

**Individual strategies:** Every day you will be offered specific strategies that you can try out in your own mentoring practice. These will be summarised in one page or less and will be accompanied by the following features.

**Strategy in action:** Every strategy will be illustrated by an exercise, an example of a scenario or a conversation which will show you how the idea might look in practice, and under what kind of circumstances it might be used. Of course, in order to keep things punchy and digestible, these examples are inevitably abbreviated versions of what might happen in a real mentoring conversation.

**A spot of theory:** While every effort has been made to try and keep this book focused on practical, accessible and easy-to-digest strategies for busy classroom teachers, we recognise that it is sometimes useful to have an idea of the theories underpinning some of the practices described. You may want to do additional reading for your own personal development, or you may need references for additional studies that you are undertaking. So throughout every chapter you will find 'A spot of theory' features. These will briefly signpost you to further reading and sources of information on the concepts discussed.

**If you only try one thing from this chapter, try this:** Towards the end of each chapter there is a recommendation of which strategy it would be most important for you to have a go at. Knowing how busy you are, we thought it might be useful, if you only have time to try one thing, to have some guidance as to what that might be. However, you are of course free to try out whatever strategies suit you best, or even to invent new ones of your own!

**Checklist:** At the end of the chapter you will be given a checklist of the strategies covered that day, so that you can record the results of trying them out for yourself, and note whether you would use them again. There is even room to record the success or otherwise of your own strategies.

In addition to all this you will find cartoons and diagrams, some of which help to summarise the various aspects of mentoring practice being presented, and others of which are included merely to provide some light relief.

It only remains to say that, if you are reading this book, it is likely that you are already a busy classroom teacher and therefore performing a challenging, occasionally frustrating, but potentially hugely rewarding role. Well, as a mentor, you are about to take on another role which, though distinct from teaching, is every bit as challenging and rewarding. You will be giving the colleagues with whom you work the gift of a dedicated, safe space in which to reflect upon and develop their classroom practice, and you will also be bestowing on them the combined benefits of your undivided attention, your empathetic understanding, your perceptive questioning and your respect for their expertise and resourcefulness in overcoming the changing professional challenges they must face. In so doing, you will help them to be happier and more successful in their work, help raise the performance of your school or college, and learn a lot about yourself into the bargain.

Happy mentoring!

# DAY 1: What is mentoring?

*A learning dialogue with another individual which helps you to develop the skills, knowledge and/or confidence to identify and achieve changes you want to make.*

Once qualified, your continuing professional development will be a mix of in-service training courses and what we loosely call 'learning on the job'. Where does mentoring fit in?

Mentoring is much better at helping you tap into existing knowledge and expertise than it is at transmitting entirely new skills. Conversely, formal training courses, while a cost-effective way of communicating new know-how, are notoriously prone to poor retention and application of learning after the event. As for learning on the job, well, we are a bit inclined to assume it just happens automatically, as if by osmosis.

You only really learn as a result of *reflective practice*. You must think critically about both on-the-job experiences and classroom training in a way which enables you to derive clear insights about your current ideas, practices or behaviours and decide what you want to do differently. That is where mentoring comes in. It is brilliant at helping you to reflect, formulate insights and make changes as a result.

What is more, most of us have encountered it already. Asked to think of a person who has impacted most positively on their development and say what they did, a room full of teachers will readily cite a host of things that sound much like mentoring.

* They had faith in me, even when I lacked faith in myself.
* They took the time and trouble to listen to and understand me.
* They challenged me.
* They offered me a different/broader view of things.
* They supported and reassured me.
* They gave me helpful feedback.

Because so much informal mentoring goes on, not just in schools but in all walks of life, we can sometimes underestimate the expertise, structure and discipline required to do mentoring well. Today's strategies, and indeed the rest of this book, aim to give you exactly that!

## Today's strategies

1. Horses for courses
2. A conversation Jim, but not as we know it
3. No guru, no teacher
4. Lose the monkey

# 1. Horses for courses

The first strategy is to determine what kind of help your mentee needs from you and adjust your mentoring to fit. And you must do this continually, as their needs change. At the same time, there are some critical boundaries which you need to observe. The diagram opposite will help to explain this.

From the diagram, you can see that great mentoring encompasses both supportive and challenging interventions, as well as varying degrees of directiveness, up to and including giving feedback or sharing experience. As a mentor, you move around these dimensions according to the needs of your mentees.

So, with a super-confident Newly Qualified Teacher (NQT), keen to apply what they have learned and to develop practical lesson planning strategies or behaviour management skills, you may find yourself largely in the top left-hand box of this framework, helping to stretch them via more directive interventions such as observation and feedback, asking challenging questions, and sharing alternative perspectives and strategies from your own experience.

On the other hand, you may be working with an experienced colleague, whose confidence has been undermined by new requirements or standards, or maybe a career setback, and decide that what is needed is empathetic listening, reassurance and support. They already have all the skills and knowledge to adapt to new circumstances and would rightly feel patronised by a more directive approach. This is the bottom right-hand part of the diagram.

Or maybe that brand new member of staff simply needs to understand better how things operate in her new school and needs her mentor to be a guide and role model in navigating a new environment with a different culture from what she is used to (top right of the diagram).

Your newly promoted colleague may be wondering where to find the help he needs to make the transition into a leadership role, and as a first step would benefit from some targeted reading and talking to more experienced leaders. As his mentor, you can use your network and knowledge to point him in the right direction.

The diamond shape in this diagram, however, denotes clear boundaries that as an effective mentor you will need to observe. So, what sort of behaviour might lie outside these boundaries? Working in a clockwise direction from 'Developing skills' they would include:

* teaching, instructing and providing your own solutions;
* protecting and sponsoring a young colleague;
* playing the amateur psychotherapist;
* spoon-feeding your mentee.

Rachel is mentoring Sandhya, who has recently moved to Fulbrook Primary School from a role in a comprehensive school some distance away. Initially, their conversations focused on how things worked in a much smaller school in an area with very specific challenges around ethnic mix and social deprivation. Rachel was able to recommend some useful reading about the approaches the new head had brought to the school and which had led to significant improvements in learners' performance. In recent conversations with Sandhya, however, Rachel had been careful to enquire about what sort of help would be most useful for Sandhya as they continued the mentoring. Sandhya expressed a need to understand better how she could adjust her teaching style from a secondary to a primary age group. From her own observations, Rachel is convinced that Sandhya is actually a very capable classroom teacher who seems, in a matter of weeks, to have developed an effective relationship and approach with her class. She wonders, therefore, whether her unease has less to do with her 'technical' abilities to engage with this different age group, and more to do with a lack of confidence clouding her ability to see how well she is doing.

**Rachel:**

" So, how have you been feeling about your teaching since we had our last chat around your ideas for the local history project?

**Sandhya:**

" Okay, I suppose, but I'm still not sure whether the canal stuff is going to keep the interest of nine and ten year olds.

**Rachel:**

" Really? What makes you say that?

**Sandhya:**

" Well, I'm just constantly aware of what a massive transition this is for me, and I don't want to mess it up.

**Rachel:**

" From what I've seen and heard, the kids seem really engaged in what you've been doing so far, and your assessment of how to pitch things for this age group has sounded spot on. Why don't we review the last few weeks and talk about what has gone well? It may be worth re-examining your assumptions about this transition you're making...

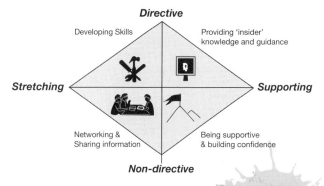

**A Spot of Theory**

*How mentoring helps (adapted from Clutterbuck, 1985).*

## 2. A conversation Jim, but not as we know it

So, how do you actually conduct these helpful discussions? You want it to feel relaxed, but you also need for it to be purposeful and result in some sort of outcome. Picture it as a journey that you and your mentee need to take: a journey of reflection.

Most of us rarely get the time and space in which to really reflect on our experiences during the hurly-burly of the school day. Ask most teachers when they have their best ideas and they'll probably say in the shower, or when walking the dog, or driving to work, or mowing the lawn. This is because our minds generally reflect better when we feel relaxed and are not full of the hundred-and-one tasks we are trying to juggle. So before we even embark on our journey, we need to relax. Ask your mentee how they are, how their week has been. Engage in a bit of social chit-chat.

Next, we need to decide where we are going, why, and how we might best get there. This means finding out what your mentee wants to get out of the conversation, and what would be a good outcome for them in the time available. You will also want to find out some context, why this is important to them and what is at stake. Finally, you need to understand what sort of help they want you to provide. Think back to our diagram above.

Now you both know where you are going, the reflective journey begins with questions which help your mentee to reflect on their experiences. They will find it easy to give you an *account* of what has been happening. Your job is to ask questions which force them to reflect on the *reasons why* things are as they are, and what part they have played in this, knowingly or unknowingly.

This exploration should help your mentee to arrive at some insight, so the next stage on the journey is helping them articulate this insight and think about what it means for them.

From here you can move to asking your mentee about what different choices they might make and what different strategies they might try out in the future. The aim here is to help your mentee be creative and consider more than just the first thing that pops into their head.

Finally, you arrive at your destination, which is your mentee's commitment to some clear plan as to what they are actually going to go away and do. So, to recap:

- check-in and relax;
- agree where, why and how;
- explore and reflect;
- articulate insights;
- possible choices for change;
- commitment to act.

*I think we've entered reflective space Jim*

Imagine you are mentoring a colleague (it might help to picture someone specific), and think of a realistic issue that they might bring to a mentoring session. With this in mind, for each of the six stages listed above try to think of what sort of questions you might ask. Try to stick to asking questions. To help you along, there is a suggested example question for each stage. See how many more you can think of.

## Check-in and relax

66 *Come on in. How have things been with you since we last spoke?*

## Agree where, why and how

66 *Where do you want to get to in the next hour or so, in order for you to feel it's been a worthwhile conversation?*

## Explore and reflect

66 *So, can you think of a specific example of this? What worked well for you on that occasion?*

## Articulate insights

66 *Given what you've just said, how are things looking to you now?*

## Possible choices for change

66 *If you had all the time and resources you wanted, what would you do differently?*

## Commitment to act

66 *So, of all these potential ideas, which do you think would be the best place to start?*

Once you have exhausted all your ideas for questions under these headings, consider whether there might be any other final things you want to ask before closing the session down. An example could be:

66 *Is there anything more I could do to help you implement this successfully?*

**A Spot of Theory**

*You will have already come across the concept of the learning cycle initially developed back in the seventies by David A. Kolb. This idea, that we all learn essentially by reflecting on our experiences and then drawing conclusions from this and altering our behaviour accordingly, underpins most models of the mentoring process.*

---

# 3. No guru, no teacher

One of the major challenges for anyone coming new to mentoring is resisting the temptation to analyse the situation, 'solve the problem', construct their own solutions and offer these to the mentee. This challenge is greater for teachers because you will be mentoring someone who does the same job as you, and therefore you will inevitably have your own answers to whatever it is they want to work on. Furthermore, many mentees will try to manoeuvre you into simply giving them answers. They may be anxious NQTs keen to suck you dry of bright ideas, or experienced colleagues wanting to blame your daft idea when everything goes pear-shaped. Either way, you will need to firmly, but supportively, resist such temptations. But how?

A.  **Ask, don't tell:** It is much harder to provide solutions if you stick to questions. Good questions encourage reflection and make your mentee think. Of course, you could just keep asking *'Have you tried...?'* but hopefully you will realise how very annoying this is (especially if you have ever been on the receiving end of it!).

B.  **Listen, don't speak:** It is also difficult to provide solutions when you keep your mouth shut, so make sure you spend most of the time listening. Remember this is about helping the mentee learn how to reflect and develop for themselves, so it's important to get comfortable with long silences!

C.  **Understand, don't solve:** If you focus your attention on trying to understand, in greater and greater depth, the situation or experience your mentee is describing, rather than searching for solutions, you will not only avoid telling them what to do, but actually help them deepen their understanding and awareness as well. This way they will arrive at insights of their own.

So, as an experienced practitioner, what is wrong with you simply helping your colleagues with a few of your bright ideas? Here are a few points to consider.

- Everyone has a different personality and style. What works for you may not work for others.
- We are all more committed to actions and changes we have come up with ourselves.
- We retain knowledge longer when we have worked it out ourselves.
- By coming up with our own answers we not only learn, but we also learn *how* to learn.
- Nobody likes a smart-alec.

## A Spot of Theory

*In her book* Adults Learning *(Open University Press, 2001), Jenny Rogers has some good advice for avoiding 'advice in disguise' questions. She suggests that questions beginning with*

*Is / Isn't; Was / Wasn't; Does / Doesn't or
Have / Haven't; Has / Hasn't; Must / Mustn't*

*almost always end with 'advice in disguise' and should therefore be avoided.*

Take a look at the questions you came up with for each stage of the mentoring conversation. Compare these with the suggestions below.

**Check-in and relax**

- *How are things with you these days?*
- *What's been going on since we last spoke?*
- *How's your week been so far?*

**Agree where, why and how**

- *What do you want to talk about today?*
- *What would you like to get out of this discussion?*
- *Why is this important? How does it fit in with your longer term development?*
- *What would make for a good outcome for you this session?*
- *How can I best help you?*

**Explore and reflect**

- *Could you talk me through an example of what you mean?*
- *So what do you think went well/not so well here?*
- *What do think might have been the reason for that?*
- *How do you think other people felt about that?*
- *Can you think of an occasion when this went better for you?*
- *What was different about that?*

**Articulate insights**

- *So what has that all told you?*
- *How do you see things differently now in the light of that?*
- *Are there any conclusions we could draw here?*

**Possible choices for change**

- *What have you got control over here?*
- *What could you do differently? What else?*
- *If you had endless resources what would you do?*
- *How would you proceed if you were feeling at your most confident?*

**Commitment to act**

- *So, which of these options seems easiest/comes first/gives you the best result?*
- *What can you do without any outside help?*
- *When and how will you go about this?*
- *How committed do you feel to this action?*
- *What might get in the way of you doing this?*
- *What else could I do to help?*

# 4. Lose the monkey

One of the common side-effects of the natural inclination to problem-solve is a sense of responsibility for the outcomes of your mentoring. Because teachers and school leaders spend their working lives taking the problems raised by their students and colleagues and doing their best to resolve them, you may well find yourself feeling this same sense of responsibility when listening to your mentee. But taking this monkey onto your own back is unhelpful for several reasons.

- You focus your attention and energy on trying to find a solution, instead of helping your mentee do *their* best thinking.

- You get anxious and this stops you listening properly and following the mentee's train of thought.

- You may jump to solutions and fail to explore fully the context and assumptions behind the mentee's experiences.

To avoid this happening, you need to give yourself permission to let go of a couple of things.

A.  **Let go of the responsibility for the mentee's actions**. After all, you have no direct control over what your mentee does as a result of the conversations you have. Their actions and their development are rightly their own responsibility. What you should feel responsible for is using all your skills as a mentor to help them do their best thinking about whatever challenge they are facing, and then build the clarity and confidence to do something about it.

B.  **Let go of the responsibility for being in control**. The best mentoring is a conversation between two equal partners who both bring skills and knowledge and insights to the discussion. It is true that part of your skills as a mentor will be structuring the conversation, but this is a process two people participate in, not something that an expert does to an unsuspecting stooge. So, feel free to admit if you're a bit lost, or cannot think what to ask next, or aren't sure if you're being helpful. This stops you worrying about the perfection of your process and allows you to concentrate on your mentee.

### A Spot of Theory

*Terri Scandura, an American academic, has researched and written extensively on dependency and other dangers inherent in mentoring. Try reading her article, 'Dysfunctional Mentoring Relationships and Outcomes' in* Journal of Management *(1998). (See Further reading for full reference.)*

Craig has been asked to mentor Jackie, an NQT in the English department of a large academy school. She comes to him concerned about the number of hours she is working.

**Craig:**

" So, Jackie, not the first time we've chatted about this, as I recall…

**Jackie:**

" Yeah, I could really do with some help. I seem to be spending all the hours God sends on marking and lesson planning, and it's really stressing me out and leaving me feeling wiped out the whole time.

**Craig:**

" That must be really distressing for you. What sort of help would be most useful from me?

**Jackie:**

" Well just some tips and tricks really around how you handle this. Maybe some examples of your lesson plans. Also, it would really help if you could double-mark some papers for me just to help me check whether I'm applying marking criteria correctly.

**Craig:**

" Hmmm… Well I'm normally comfortable with doing a bit of second marking Jackie, but it strikes me that I've done a fair bit of that for you already. Why do you think the marking is still taking you so long?

**Jackie:**

" I just keep going over scripts again and again to make sure I'm not being unfair to anyone. I'm nervous about mucking up a kid's chances by getting it wrong.

**Craig:**

" Every time I've second-marked stuff for you, I've been hard-pressed to find any errors, so what evidence do you have for supposing you might be getting it wrong?

**Jackie:**

" Well… no evidence as such… I just worry…

**Craig:**

" Remember when we talked about how this mentoring lark works and how it wasn't helpful in the long term if I did stuff for you or just handed out solutions?

**Jackie:**

" Yes, but surely you're here partly to help me improve my skills?

**Craig:**

" Absolutely, but from what I've seen, your approach to assessment and, for that matter, lesson planning, is very proficient. How would you feel about an experiment? Try just going through the kids' work once or twice, mark it and then leave it alone. Try it for just a couple of weeks and we'll talk about how that went.

**Jackie**:

" Well I suppose I could try it…

**Craig:**

" I think you'll be surprised. Now, let's move onto lesson planning. Tell me how you're going about it now and why you think it's not working…

**If you only try one thing from this chapter, try this***

**Checklist**

Use this to keep a record of what worked well for you and what didn't. Not every strategy will suit every school, or perhaps be practicable. There's a line at the bottom for you to add your own strategy, if it's not already included.

| Strategy | Tried it with... | On...(date) | It worked | It didn't work | Worth trying again? |
|---|---|---|---|---|---|
| 1. Horses for courses | | | | | |
| 2. A conversation Jim, but not as we know it | | | | | |
| **3. No guru, no teacher***<br>A. Ask, don't tell<br>B. Listen, don't speak<br>C. Understand, don't solve | | | | | |
| 4. Lose the monkey<br>A. Let go of the responsibility for mentee's action<br>B. Let go of the responsibility for being in control | | | | | |
| Your own strategy? | | | | | |

# DAY 2: Making mentoring work well

Now you know what mentoring is and how it works, what is to stop you simply telling staff that you are implementing this wonderful process across your school and then letting them get on with helping each other to develop and grow? Well, it is true that mentoring often happens in schools on an entirely informal and voluntary basis, and it is also true that these kinds of mentoring partnerships can be very successful. However, this ignores some of the things that have gone badly wrong when mentoring has been poorly implemented in schools. In the introduction to this book we looked at some of the positive results of mentoring uncovered by a big piece of research into the mentoring of new teachers. Unfortunately, the same research also found the following examples of unintended consequences.

* **Mentors experiencing:**
  * the burden of increased workload;
  * feelings of insecurity, threat or inadequacy;
  * a sense of isolation.
* **Mentees experiencing:**
  * insufficient support;
  * increased pressure and anxiety;
  * a feeling of being bullied;
  * not being sufficiently challenged;
  * insufficient responsibility or freedom to innovate;
  * technical skills development, not learning skills development.

* **Schools and colleges, as a result, experiencing:**
  * perpetuation of conventional as opposed to innovative practices;
  * a lack of challenge and reform.

So what is going wrong here, and how can you avoid it? The answers lie in the following key elements:

* defining the purpose of mentoring and the roles within it;
* having the conditions in place which support and encourage good mentoring;
* integrating the process into how the school works;
* giving staff the skills to undertake this well;
* maintaining momentum and continuing development.

Today's strategies are designed to ensure that you get these things right when you implement mentoring in your school.

## Today's strategies

1. Why, oh why, oh why?
2. The right stuff
3. Hearts and minds
4. Bite-sized learning and do-it-yourself CPD

# 1. Why, oh why, oh why?

## Be clear what the mentoring is for (and be clear what you are for!)

Let's assume you have been appointed 'cheerleader' for this new kind of staff development process and are wondering where on earth to start. You could be a member of the management team, or a teacher with particular responsibility for staff development. In an FE college, you may even be part of the human resources department. Hopefully, you have not been the victim of a rigged lottery or cruel joke, but have a real enthusiasm for and commitment to the concept of mentoring. As 'mentoring champion' your role is to co-ordinate discussions and decisions about how it will operate in your school. Here are just some of the things you may need to do.

- Promote the concept of mentoring and encourage continuing commitment to it.
- Ensure that mentoring is well integrated with other staff development processes.
- Co-ordinate key decisions about the mentoring, such as objectives, evaluation criteria, and matching and training of potential participants.
- Arrange or even deliver briefing and training sessions to staff.
- Evaluate how well it is working for staff and ensure continuous improvement.

However, job number one is to help the school determine *what the mentoring is for and what the roles of mentor and mentee are*. Failure to answer this simple question first will make it very difficult to answer many of the subsequent questions you will run into; questions like:

- How can we justify the time spent on mentoring?
- How will we know that mentoring is helping staff in the way we intended?
- How should we position this with staff to ensure they engage with it?
- What kind of training and continuing support will mentors and mentees need?

Let us assume for the moment that your main objective is to help staff develop their skills and knowledge, not just in the classroom, but in other contexts too, such as management and leadership. All well and good, but what about considering some of these other outcomes?

- supporting staff in coping with aspects of the job they may find stressful;
- enhancing or maintaining motivation and morale, thus improving staff retention;
- helping career planning and preparing staff for major career transitions;
- improving the attractiveness of the school/college to new recruits;
- supporting diversity policies by promoting better mutual understanding between different groups of staff.

You also need to think about whether this is for all staff or a select few, whether it is intended to perpetuate a 'winning formula' or encourage new and creative approaches, and whether you want it to focus on short-term performance, long-term transitions, or both. Arriving at a clear vision in answer to these sorts of questions will enable you to decide what you want from your mentors and how much you want mentees to drive the process.

As mentoring champion, Neerja is explaining to her head teacher what she thinks the purpose and role of mentors should be.

**Neerja:**

" It's important that all staff buy in to this, Alistair. We need to be sending a message that continuing professional development is a requirement for everyone, not just newly qualifieds, or fast-track stars, or under-performers, but _all_ staff; you and the senior team included.

**Alistair:**

" Yeah, but hang on. Who's going to mentor me?

**Neerja:**

" Someone external maybe? A governor? A head from another school in the network? Or maybe even one of your senior team? The point is, if we see mentoring as supporting staff as well as developing them, we not only improve classroom practice and raise school performance, but we create a better working environment as well. If this is seen as some smart-alec super teacher telling me how to do my job better, or enforcing a raft of standard practices, we'll just switch people off. We want mentors who question and stretch people, give them the confidence to try out their _own_ new ideas and encourage innovation.

**Alistair:**

" So how will we link it to the performance appraisal? Will I get to see reports from the mentors?

**Neerja:**

" I reckon we should keep the two things entirely separate. Don't you think people will engage more honestly and enthusiastically with mentoring if they see it as primarily to help them be happier in their job, rather than there to assess them, or 'fix' them in some way?

### A Spot of Theory

In her book, Implementing Mentoring Schemes (Butterworth Heinemann, 2002), Nadine Klasen provides some interesting statistics about the difference between well and poorly implemented mentoring. In well-planned and maintained schemes, 85 per cent of all pairs report significant mutual learning, whereas in poorly planned schemes this success rate can be 30 per cent or less.

'I think he may have the wrong idea of what this mentoring lark is really about'

## 2. The right stuff

### Do you have what it takes to be a mentor?

It may be that your school is one of those adopting a very inclusive approach to all this; one where everyone should be trained in mentoring and people form mentoring partnerships entirely informally without any involvement or co-ordination from the school itself. Let us be clear, there is not necessarily anything wrong with this. It may be exactly what suits the culture and circumstances of your school best.

However, if the process of becoming a mentor needs to be more selective, then you will be faced with the question of what makes for a good or bad mentor. You may also need to consider what makes for a good mentee.

So here are some of the qualities you do NOT want, followed by an idea of what questions you might ask yourself or others in order to check if you or they have the 'right stuff'.

#### No one wants a mentor who...

* loves nothing more than to talk about themselves and their accomplishments;
* believes that they have learned pretty much all they need to know;
* believes there is generally only one right way of doing things;
* wouldn't want to risk upsetting a colleague by giving them negative feedback;
* wants to 'give back' by sharing all their wisdom;
* gets embarrassed when you talk about your feelings.

#### No one wants a mentee who...

* is only being mentored because he thinks it is what is expected;
* never really thinks about her professional practice and what works;
* thinks that she can suck her mentor dry of all their tips and tricks rather than develop their own approaches;
* cannot be bothered to think carefully before a mentoring session about what he wants to get out of it;
* sees asking for help as a sign of failure or weakness;
* acts the helpless victim who just wants to be given the 'answer'.

### A Spot of Theory

*In his influential book,* Everyone Needs a Mentor *(CIPD, 2004), David Clutterbuck has a whole chapter on selecting and matching mentors and mentees, including a description of the 'mentor from hell'.*

Porchester College of Further Education is piloting a mentoring programme for staff, initially just within the Building Trades Department. Aidan, as programme co-ordinator, is charged with establishing a group of six mentors, and Ron has expressed an interest in being one of them.

**Aidan:**

" *Okay Ron, I thought it might be an idea to chat about this mentoring pilot over a quick coffee, just to fill you in on what's expected and talk about whether it would be a good thing for you to do.*

**Ron:**

" *Absolutely. Fire away.*

**Aidan:**

" *I guess the first question is what sparked your interest?*

**Ron:**

" *Well, you know, I've always been like a bit of a father figure to these younger lecturers. 15 years in the trade and then 15 years teaching. I think I just about know all there is to know about this stuff by now. Also, I've been thinking about applying for the Assistant Head of Department job. This kind of thing on the CV wouldn't do any harm.*

**Aidan:**

" *I see, and what do you think are the main benefits you could bring to people as a mentor?*

**Ron:**

" *Well, though I say so myself, just years of experience and, I suppose, a certain wisdom. There aren't many problems they're going to come across that I couldn't offer them some way out of. I sort of feel it's time I shared some of what I've learned over the years.*

**Aidan:**

" *And what are you hoping to learn from the mentoring?*

**Ron:**

" *What am I hoping to learn? How do you mean?*

**Aidan:**

" *Well, you know, practices and technologies change and improve. Do you think you could learn from some of the younger folk coming into the job?*

**Ron:**

" *Possibly... I hadn't really thought about it, I suppose.*

**Aidan:**

" *And what if a mentee wasn't really after improving their teaching as such, but was maybe letting the job get on top of them a bit and needed to talk to someone about it?*

**Ron:**

" *I think I'd send them to the nurse...*

**Aidan:**

" *Yes... we haven't actually employed a nurse at the college since 2005, Ron...*

# 3. Hearts and minds

For mentoring to work well you will need to get buy-in, which means talking to those who will be mentors and mentees about what *they* want the process to do for them, and how it should be structured. People do not want to feel shoehorned into yet another initiative. And that is not the only thing that might demotivate your fledgling mentors and mentees. Here are some others:

- detailed record-keeping and reporting;
- onerous and too-frequent monitoring;
- forced pairing of mentors and mentees;
- having a mentor whether you want one or not;
- imposing blanket standards and objectives on mentees and ignoring *their* learning agenda.

Mentoring is a process requiring two consenting parties who can see something in it for *them*. You cannot do it by stealth or by force. And yet some overall co-ordination can be helpful. If you just step back entirely and let people get on with it, the school will be unable to promote a clear purpose for the mentoring, properly train and support mentors and mentees, or evaluate how well it is working. What is more, there is a good chance that some people will lose out in the general free-for-all.

The trick here is to create the infrastructure to support mentors and mentees, but try to avoid 'Big Brother' bureaucracy. At the heart of achieving this delicate balance is the tricky question of how mentors and mentees are matched up. Forced matching by you as mentoring champion requires encyclopaedic knowledge of every staff member's personality and preferences. Even in a small school, where this may be possible, it still

removes initiative and control from the mentee. You could, of course, just leave mentees to choose their own mentor, or vice versa, but you may need to specify a maximum number of mentees per mentor or this could result in a very uneven use of resources. An alternative approach, particularly for larger schools and colleges, is to offer prospective mentees a shortlist of two or three potential mentors and then allow them to make a final choice. If you work in a very large institution, where people know each other less well, try asking mentors and mentees to provide a brief biography about their background, career and interests.

Finally, you need to ensure that mentoring is properly integrated into the range of professional development tools (including inset days, external courses, coaching, additional responsibilities etc) which are discussed as part of any staff member's personal development plan. Key points are:

- it is seen as a process from which successful teachers and managers benefit;
- staff enter into it willingly, as part of their agreed development plan;
- learning goals of the mentoring complement and reflect learning goals from other development processes;
- mentoring is used for what it is good at (see Day 1), and not as an alternative to more appropriate skills training mechanisms.

So, having consulted with colleagues and agreed the appropriate degree of co-ordination required for your school or college, how do you then maintain people's commitment and enthusiasm?

- Engage in some form of evaluation and reporting back (more on this in Day 7!).

- Keep an eye out for articles or new books about mentoring and circulate information about these to mentors and mentees.

- Start every inset day with a brief account from a mentee about how it has helped them.

- Provide opportunities for those acting as mentors to support each other by sharing successful strategies or challenges encountered (given appropriate ground rules about confidentiality, of course).

- Ensure the head teacher and leadership team talk about mentoring when reviewing staff development. Ideally get them to talk about their *own* mentoring experiences.

- Ensure that experienced and highly regarded members of staff are seen to benefit from mentoring just as much as anyone else.

- Have a 'celebration event' once a year where mentors and mentees get to mark the success of their work together. Use this opportunity to communicate specific achievements from the mentoring evaluation feedback.

" My profile says GSOH, NSA and N/D, but I still didn't get picked"

**A Spot of Theory**

*Elaine Cox, in her 2005 article, 'For Better, For Worse: The Matching Process in Formal Mentoring Schemes', concludes that external interference in mentor–mentee matching may be altogether unnecessary. Her research indicates that mentee needs may not fully emerge until the partnership is well under way, and that rapport is often built in spontaneous and random ways during the relationship which matching processes cannot possibly anticipate. Our efforts are therefore best spent on training mentors to recognise and build on these spontaneous moments.*

# 4. Bite-sized learning and do-it-yourself CPD

Experience suggests that a number of short training inputs over six to nine months can be preferable to just one extended session at the start of the mentoring process. The reason for this is two-fold.

* Shorter workshop sessions make it easier to retain knowledge and mentors can relate more easily to some of the skills training once they have experienced mentoring someone for real.

* Having a series of supportive training inputs can help maintain interest and momentum, as well as giving mentors a chance to bring 'real-life' successes and challenges to the discussion.

For your school, the precious *inset* day may make it easier to plan and get supply cover. Nevertheless, if there are more creative ways you can accommodate several shorter workshops, you will undoubtedly find this more effective.

What kind of topics does the training need to cover? Here are some suggestions.

A. Outline of scheme purpose and structure.

B. Who can be a mentor/mentee, and how are they matched?

C. What mentoring is and how it works.

D. Contracting, boundaries and confidentiality.

E. Structuring the conversation to make it purposeful.

F. Techniques and skills (eg listening, questioning).

G. Reviewing how things are going and making improvements.

H. Motivation and ethical considerations.

I. What happens when mentoring comes to an end.

In a brief, introductory workshop you need only focus on what mentors need in order to get the ball rolling (probably topics A−E above). The rest can wait until they have had a few real-life mentoring conversations. You should definitely provide training to prospective mentees as well (some people will find themselves in both roles, after all) and you should seriously consider training mentors and mentees together. It helps to promote transparency and trust.

One final thought: No training session is complete without the opportunity to practise the process in a safe environment. It doesn't have to be a role play. Mentees can absolutely be themselves and talk about real issues, but if you miss this out you will be losing the one element that participants always say is the most useful.

One way of incorporating continuing training and support, without expensive external resources, is to encourage and enable mentors to spend time sharing experiences, challenges and successful strategies in small reflective practice groups on a regular basis (maybe once a term). These groups could be self-managed or facilitated by the mentoring champion.

Sonia, Ben, Zadie and Gurbinder have decided to support each other as mentors by getting together occasionally as an informal learning set. At their initial meeting they are trying to work out how this will operate.

**Ben:**

" Okay, so what do we need to sort out at this stage do you reckon?

**Zadie:**

" Well, I was jotting down a list over breakfast this morning, and I came up with frequency, facilitation, format and first challenges.

**Sonia:**

" Think you missed out fag breaks! Care to elucidate on your alliteration?

**Zadie:**

" Yeah, sure. We need to decide how often it will be practical to meet up. My vote would be probably once a term. Do we need someone to facilitate discussions? I reckon not, provided we agree on a fairly standard format. And finally, do we want to share some initial challenges we have encountered already in the mentoring, before we finish today, just to test out how useful this kind of peer support thing might be?

**Ben:**

" That's really helpful, Zadie, thanks. Do we have any ideas about a standard format for these sessions?

**Gurbinder:**

" I don't know if it's the same sort of thing, but when I worked in industry we had action learning sets. They always started with everyone just checking in and briefly saying what they'd been up to. Then we built an informal agenda with rough timings, by checking round who had a specific issue or challenge to discuss. Each person who wanted to would be kind of coached by the rest of the group, and then we'd wrap up with a summary of learnings from the session...

**A Spot of Theory**

In their review of some 300 research-based articles, covering mentoring in education, medicine and business contexts, the Australian academics Ehrich, Hansford and Tennent (2004) conclude that mentoring, despite its enormous potential to generate personal growth and professional development, also has a 'dark side', and they highlighted several critical issues to be addressed in order to minimise the likelihood of problems. Foremost among these is the training of mentors.

**Checklist**

Use this to keep a record of what worked well for you and what didn't. Not every strategy will suit every school, or perhaps be practicable. There's a line at the bottom for you to add your own strategy, if it's not already included.

| Strategy | Tried it with... | On...(date) | It worked | It didn't work | Worth trying again? |
|---|---|---|---|---|---|
| **1. Why, oh why, oh why?*** | | | | | |
| 2. The right stuff | | | | | |
| 3. Hearts and minds | | | | | |
| 4. Bite-sized learning and do-it-yourself CPD | | | | | |
| Your own strategy? | | | | | |

# DAY 3: Building the partnership

You now hopefully have a clearer idea of how mentoring works, what it does well and how you can start to structure these conversations in order to make them productive and meaningful.

Before we go any further though, we must address a challenging series of questions which lie at the heart of successful mentoring:

*Why on earth should this person engage willingly in these conversations with <u>you</u>, share their innermost hopes and fears with <u>you</u>, admit their mistakes and celebrate their successes with <u>you</u>, and accept honest feedback from <u>you</u>?*

Well, you can tell yourself that it's because you are an Advanced Skills Teacher, or because you are deputy head, or because the head has told everyone they've got to have a mentor, but you know, in your heart of hearts, that none of these answers really fly, don't you?

No, imagine yourself as the mentee. The reason you will do all these things is that you trust and respect your mentor, feel safe discussing with them sensitive and personal insights into your own skills, knowledge and experience, and you are confident that they have your best interests at heart.

In today's chapter we are going to take a look at how you set about building a partnership which feels like this. But first here are some things that might get in the way.

* **Power difference:** Like it or not, if you are more senior, this power dynamic will impinge on trust. Good mentors find ways of overcoming this.

* **Appraisal and assessment of staff:** This is part of your job as a school leader, but one which may make your mentee think twice about speaking openly.

* **'Compulsory' mentoring:** Mentoring works best as a relationship entered into willingly by two consenting individuals. Forcing it on someone puts up an immediate barrier to trust.

* **Insufficient time:** Rushed mentoring communicates a lack of respect and will undermine the partnership.

* **Lack of privacy:** If your mentee cannot talk to you in private or they are worried about confidentiality, they will find it hard to open up to you.

## Today's strategies

1. The rules of the game

2. Safety first

3. Knowing me, knowing you

4. Stand by me

# 1. The rules of the game

The idea of a conversation having rules may seem off-putting to you at first, but consider this: you are asking a colleague to share with you openly their thoughts about their own performance, their future career, their feelings about their job, and perhaps their relationships with other colleagues, learners or parents. If you were them, wouldn't you want some guidelines as to how this is going to work?

So, right at the start of your mentoring, you need to get some clear agreement with your mentee about what the ground rules are that will govern these conversations. Here are the kind of topics you will want to cover.

## Confidentiality

The baseline here is that nothing spoken about in your mentoring sessions will be revealed to anyone else without your joint agreement. You cannot, as a mentor, collude in illegality or rule breaking, especially around child protection issues, and you will want to reserve the option to breach confidentiality if you feel your mentee themselves might be at risk of harm. But other than these two, thankfully rare, exceptions, the more complete your joint commitment to confidentiality can be, the greater the degree of trust you will engender.

## Boundaries

What are the limits of the help you can provide as a mentor? (Remember the framework from Day 1?) Are there any topics your mentee would prefer *not* to include in your conversations?

## Expectations

Be clear about how mentoring works, what it is realistic for your mentee to expect from you (eg not answers and solutions) and what the process will require of them.

## Mutual responsibilities

Include things like respecting each other's time and sticking to commitments, especially about actions occurring as a result of mentoring conversations.

## Evaluating progress

How will you keep track of whether the mentoring is achieving what you both want it to? Inevitably this will require...

## Giving and receiving feedback

Give each other permission to do this honestly, and discuss how you each prefer to receive it.

## How and when to meet

How often? How long? What time of day? Where feels comfortable?

## Note-taking and records

If you decide these are helpful, agree how you will keep them private, and what happens to them after the mentoring finishes.

## No-fault divorce

You may fail to 'click', despite your best efforts, so give each other permission up front to end the partnership, without recrimination, if it is proving fruitless.

Sam is having her first mentoring conversation with Amelia, an NQT who has recently started at Stanhope Primary School. They have spent some time getting to know each other better, and, before going further, Sam decides to do a bit of contracting…

**Sam:**

" *Thanks for that Amelia. It's been lovely finding out a bit more about each other. If it's okay with you, I'd now just like to turn our attention to how we want this mentoring relationship to work. I've generally found it helpful to agree a few simple ground rules, just so you feel comfortable talking about things and I am able to provide the most appropriate help. Does that sound sensible?*

**Amelia:**

" *Yes, sure. What kind of things did you mean?*

**Sam:**

" *Well, probably most importantly, you need to know from me that what is said in these conversations we have will be kept entirely confidential between the two of us, unless we agree otherwise. The only things I can't promise to keep to myself are obviously any kind of illegal behaviour, or where I think someone might be in danger of harm. But I haven't encountered either of these with a mentee yet, so I don't think we need to worry too much about them!*

**Amelia:**

" *So are these sessions not recorded in some way?*

✹ Put yourself in Sam's shoes. How would you answer this question?

**Sam:**

" *Now, I have a couple of questions for you. First of all, what are you hoping to get out of the mentoring over the next year or so?*

**Amelia:**

" *Well, I suppose I'm mainly looking to use your experience to get lots of good practical suggestions as to how I can improve my teaching and become more confident and relaxed in front of the kids.*

✹ Again, if you were Sam, how would you respond to this? Remember, the mentor is not there primarily to provide 'suggestions'.

**A Spot of Theory**

*In his book,* The Skilled Helper *(Brooks/Cole, 2002), Gerard Egan talks about a 'working charter' to help both mentor and mentee understand their roles and responsibilities.*

# 2. Safety first

Neuroscience tells us that when we are anxious or afraid, our 'fight or flight' response tends to kick in and override our brain's higher reasoning centres. In other words, we find it much easier to reflect and consider events rationally when we feel safe and relaxed. A good learning environment is a safe environment.

You have already taken a big step towards creating a safe space by agreeing the kind of ground rules outlined above. So, what else can you do? Well, aside from the obvious matter of ensuring a quiet, private location for your mentoring, where you cannot be overheard, you may also want to pick a neutral space. Remember the comment about power dynamics in the introduction to this chapter? You might even want to consider the benefit of conducting a session somewhere more informal off school premises, if you feel this would break the ice and enable you both to feel more relaxed.

Given the importance of trust in creating a safe space, it is also instructive to consider what generates (and therefore what undermines) trust.

**Competence:** A mentee will feel safer in the hands of a mentor who knows what they are doing, so hone your mentoring skills.

**Integrity:** We tend to trust people who do what they say. So, as a mentor, ensure that you see through any action you have committed yourself to.

**Self-disclosure:** We trust people who ask no more of us than they do of themselves. So, if you want your mentee to feel safe talking about their challenges or development needs, be prepared to talk openly about your own.

**Partner not expert:** We are unlikely to trust a mentor who is unwilling to learn themselves. So talk to your mentee about what you hope to learn from the mentoring partnership and be sure to review this as well as the mentee's development.

**Do as I do:** If you want your mentee to feel safe and comfortable with feedback, then be a positive role model by asking for feedback about yourself. Make it clear from the off that you can benefit both as a mentor and as a colleague/school leader, from helpful feedback. This also allows you to role model how to receive and use feedback constructively.

**Show you care:** We trust people who we think have our best interests at heart, so you must demonstrate that your prime focus is to help your mentee.

Safe enough for you?

Imagine that you have had an initial meeting with a new mentee, who is an experienced colleague. You have found her a bit quiet. Maybe she has been willing to talk about what has been going on in the classroom, and about the challenges of the curriculum, but is more reluctant to open up about difficulties she has experienced or about her own feelings. She seems wary about challenging the changes being made in the school or expressing her real opinions.

You worry that you haven't really clicked and that she is unsure how much she can say in front of you, given that you are in a more senior role. You suspect she may have had some experience of mentoring before that has made her distrustful of the whole process.

✹ **What kind of things might you do in these circumstances to try and help this mentee feel safer?**

✹ **What sort of questions would you ask her?**

✹ **What questions might you ask yourself?**

Once you have thought about these questions, take a look at some of the thoughts below.

Start with the kind of questions you might ask yourself as mentor:

❝ *What am I doing or not doing that might be reinforcing the uneven power dynamic between us?*

❝ *Have I given enough of myself for her to trust me?*

❝ *Have I spent enough time on us getting to know one another?*

The questions you might want to ask your mentee would be predominantly very open-ended, in order to encourage her to talk at length and feel listened to. You could also ask for feedback about your mentoring in order to elicit some clues as to what may be getting in the way, and demonstrate your own need for development.

In order to build trust and converse as equal colleagues, you may also try recalling your own experiences of self-doubt or difficulty, and re-emphasising your desire to help.

### A Spot of Theory

*Recent research by the Chartered Institute for Personnel and Development revealed the following four qualities as key to building trust:*

✹ competence;

✹ integrity;

✹ predictability;

✹ benevolence.

# 3. Knowing me, knowing you

There is more to building a high-quality mentoring relationship than just creating a safe space in which to talk. Great mentors build a strong rapport with their mentees, which significantly enhances the quality of help they can provide. Many teachers, especially in smaller schools, tend to think they already know their colleagues pretty well (even if they don't always claim to have a strong rapport with all of them!). But often we mistake relatively superficial knowledge of colleagues' family, hobbies, holidays, pets and sporting allegiances for real understanding. Do we really know what 'makes them tick'?

When we talk about building a high-quality relationship as a mentor, we mean knowing about our mentee's values, beliefs and assumptions about the world, what enthuses and motivates them, what frustrates them, what they consider most important in life. In the best mentoring partnerships our mentees know all this about us too, because, as I've already emphasised, this kind of reciprocity helps establish trust.

How do we do this? Well, we can come right out and ask, but these can be difficult and intrusive-sounding questions to answer on the spot. So you could try asking your mentee what they feel most passionate about, or what aspects of their lives give them the greatest sense of success. You might talk about what makes them feel most frustrated or angry. If this is still too intrusive for you, you might try more playful strategies.

A. **Room 101:** Try playing the popular TV panel game and share what you dislike most about modern life, work, other people, etc. (Or if you want to be true to George Orwell's *Nineteen Eighty-Four*, talk about what you most fear!)

B. **Person you most admire:** Talking about someone we admire and why can reveal a lot about what we regard as important. It doesn't have to be someone alive now. In fact it doesn't even have to be a real person. A character from television, film or books would do just as well.

C. **What I would hate in a mentor/mentee:** Sharing thoughts about our (real or imagined) worst mentoring partner can also be a fun way of getting to know what kind of behaviour we value and what drives us mad!

Try having one of these conversations with a colleague today, and see if you discover new insights into what each other thinks.

*O.K. Tom, I think there's a difference between admiring and stalking.*

You and your mentee have been having some fun getting to know one another better. You have discovered that he hates people who are late for things. He has never been late for work, nor taken a day off sick, and doesn't see how other people should, as he sees it, 'get away' with this. He clearly has a lot of time for the head of his previous school, who was a stickler for rules, about uniform, appearance, etc and was a strict disciplinarian. However, your own observations suggest that, although inclined to be quiet and reserved, he also has a great, and often quite informal, rapport with learners.

You, on the other hand, regard yourself as someone for whom planning and structure are not the strongest suits, but whose creativity and 'have-a-go' enthusiasm enable you to perform well as a teacher and adapt easily to ever-changing demands on the profession. As a single mum, with two young children, you have hardly ever been late, but occasionally had to request some flexibility to attend key appointments, etc. You see yourself as a natural extrovert who may not always reflect carefully enough before you speak.

- What questions would you want to ask your mentee to discover more about what 'makes him tick'?

- What does this tell you about what kind of people or situations your mentee might find challenging, and what he might value unquestioningly? (Then try to answer the same questions for yourself!)

- What kind of things might you learn from each other? How might you be most helpful to your mentee?

- Are there potential sources of conflict here? What might you need to be alert to as a mentor?

**A Spot of Theory**

*In research reviewed and conducted by Eric de Haan at Ashridge Management School, a consistent result emerges across studies of psychotherapy, coaching and mentoring. One of the strongest common factors in determining successful outcomes was the quality of the relationship, especially as perceived by the mentee.*

## 4. Stand by me

Perhaps the hardest aspect of the mentoring relationship to explain is the stance or attitude you should take towards your mentee. You may have heard phrases like 'critical friend' or 'non-judgemental support' or 'unconditional positive regard', but what do these all add up to? As a mentor, you are aiming to adopt a role which balances a number of seemingly contradictory postures.

A. **You empathise but you do not sympathise:** When your mentee is describing to you a lesson with the school's most difficult class, that has got seriously out of hand, it would be easy to sympathise *('Gosh yes, that must have been awful. I'm not surprised you feel shattered, you poor thing. What a bunch of little \*\*\*\*\* they are...')*. This is what a friend would do, after all. But you are not a friend. You have a responsibility to be helpful. To do this you must retain a degree of objectivity. Someone cleverer than me observed that if someone is in a hole and you get into it with them, you immediately shorten your odds of helping them out of it. So show that you appreciate their feelings, express your desire to help, but remain sufficiently detached to help them confront what went wrong.

B. **You share feedback but you are non-judgemental:** As a teacher, much of your job, with regard to learners, is about assessment and grading and making judgements about what constitutes good, bad or indifferent work. If you are part of the school leadership team, you may even be called upon to assess colleagues in this way. However, once you put on your mentor's hat you will be more effective if you can find ways of sharing what you have observed in a neutral way, and invite your mentee to draw conclusions about what was successful and what was not.

C. **You can disagree but remain on their side:** Some of the most fruitful mentoring partnerships, from a depth of learning perspective, are between teachers with radically different views, opinions and perspectives. You may disagree with your mentee's values, politics, religious beliefs and their prediction about who will be voted out of the jungle first. However, you can still make a genuine effort to understand where these views come from, and appreciate how they affect the decisions which shape your mentee's behaviour. You work with this grain in helping your mentee achieve their goals, because the alternative is imposing your world view which, of course, will not work.

Let us assume that you are mentoring a colleague with a different personality and outlook from your own. In fact, let us take the relationship described in the last strategy above. We'll call your mentee Sadiq and we'll call you Mo. Sadiq is sharing his frustration about a particularly difficult lesson.

**Sadiq:**

" *What's so annoying is that I'd worked like stink setting up this Chemistry practical, because it all needs to be quite controlled and timing is crucial to get the best effect. The class were late out of their double maths – thanks very much Clive! – and typically dawdled their way across school. Then, I'm trying to ensure they keep in their groups, for safety reasons as much as anything, and the buggers are sneaking between benches, trying to see what results their mates are getting.*

**Mo:**

" *Yes, I can see how frustrating that must have been for you. I bet you did a fantastic job of setting it all up as well. Having worked together for a while though, I have noticed that we spend a fair bit of time talking about perfectly planned lessons that don't go to plan.*

**Sadiq:**

" *Look, I know I'm a bit of a control freak, but surely good planning is essential, especially when there are safety rules to follow?*

**Mo:**

" *Hey, nothing wrong with plans and rules per se, Sadiq, but what I'm hearing is that other people don't always follow them. So what assumptions are you making here that are proving unhelpful?*

**Sadiq:**

" *Not sure I get what you mean...*

**Mo:**

" *Well, I'm not great at planning, so things going a bit pear-shaped is normal for me. I've had to become adaptable. But you are not me, so let's think what change of approach might work for you...*

**A Spot of Theory**

*A concept that has made its way from psychotherapy to mentoring is Carl Rogers' idea of* 'unconditional positive regard': *the way in which only our acceptance of the mentee can enable them to take responsibility for their actions. See his book,* Client-centred Therapy *(Houghton Mifflin, 1951).*

**Checklist**

Use this to keep a record of what worked well for you and what didn't. Not every strategy will suit every school, or perhaps be practicable. There's a line at the bottom for you to add your own strategy, if it's not already included.

| Strategy | Tried it with... | On...(date) | It worked | It didn't work | Worth trying again? |
|---|---|---|---|---|---|
| **1. The rules of the game\*** (Agree clear ground rules. Talk about what your mentee wants to achieve and how you can help) | | | | | |
| 2. Safety first | | | | | |
| 3. Knowing me, knowing you | | | | | |
| A. Room 101 | | | | | |
| B. Person you admire | | | | | |
| C. What I would hate in a mentor/mentee | | | | | |
| 4. Stand by me | | | | | |
| A. Empathise not sympathise | | | | | |
| B. Non-judgemental feedback | | | | | |
| C. Disagree but remain on their side | | | | | |
| Your own strategy? | | | | | |

# DAY 4: Helping your mentee develop

So far, we have examined what mentoring is, how it works and what such conversations should look like. Today we will begin finding out more about the skills and techniques you draw on as a mentor by focusing on your two most important tools: listening and questioning.

One of the greatest gifts you will give your mentee is that of being really listened to by someone who pays them the respect of believing they have the capability to master whatever particular challenge they happen to be facing. You are not their boss, with one eye on what they need to get done, and your approachability compromised by the responsibility to direct and assess performance. They already have one of those. You are not their friend, feeling the need to protect and rescue them with sympathetic agreement and quick-fire solutions. They already have plenty of friends (well, hopefully). Neither are you a family member, whom they may not wish to burden with work issues. No, you are someone who will devote quality time to really understanding their particular perspective and providing objective support.

You will adopt open body language, nod, make encouraging noises, summarise, maintain regular eye contact, and all those other things you have learned on training courses. But much more than this, you will actually give them your full attention. You will stop filtering their narrative according to your values and concerns. You will stop trying to problem-solve or rescue. Instead you will tune into the feelings as well as the facts. You will notice recurring themes in the language and imagery they use, and you will become aware of what they are *not* saying.

Remember, your primary aim is to understand, so when you do speak it will almost certainly be to ask questions. The best questions are those that help your mentee do *their* best thinking by:

- clarifying aims and outcomes;
- raising self-awareness;
- encouraging deeper reflection;
- re-evaluating perspectives;
- considering alternative strategies;
- deciding what to do.

They are not those that help *you* solve the puzzle.

## Today's strategies

1. Watch yourself
2. If you only have a hammer
3. Let silence be your friend
4. Dig deep

# 1. Watch yourself

One of the tricky things about mentoring is that you have to master a range of skills and use these in a structured and purposeful conversation while maintaining a zen-like level of attention on your mentee. But you also have to combine this with a degree of self-monitoring, to ensure that you are indeed doing all these things and getting better at doing them. This ability to monitor your behaviour is crucial to your development as a mentor. Here are a few techniques based on principles you learned on Day 1:

A. **Talking ratio:** Try reflecting back on your mentoring conversations and evaluating how much time you spent talking versus how much time your mentee did. Aside perhaps from an initial meeting where you may be having to explain the process and ground rules, you should be aiming to talk no more than 20 to 30 per cent of the time, on average. If you are talking more than this, there is a good chance you are driving the agenda and/or imposing solutions. Try asking your mentee for feedback.

B. **Questions versus statements:** In a similar vein, divide your interventions into questions and statements. How much of the time are you asking as opposed to telling? Obviously hard and fast rules are misleading. But again, you generally want to be doing a lot more asking than telling. The desire to share one's own experience and expertise, for genuinely helpful reasons, can distract us from our main purpose of enabling the mentee to do their best thinking.

C. **Open to closed:** So, are there any other 'triggers' you should watch out for? For example, if you find yourself moving from open questions (see Strategy 2 below) to increasingly closed questions, you may, albeit inadvertently, be adopting a more diagnostic approach and homing in on your own solution to the issue being addressed by your mentee. This can also manifest itself in an increasing frequency of questions, gradually transforming a relaxed, contemplative space into a police interrogation.

**A Spot of Theory**

*In their book,* Coaching and Mentoring at Work *(Open University Press, 2007), Mary Connor and Julia Pokora refer to diagnostic listening (as typified by a doctor asking about symptoms to identify a patient's condition and recommend treatment) and how this differs from the active listening required of mentors.*

Let's take a look inside the thoughts of Krzysztof, a novice mentor, as he conducts a mentoring conversation with Mona. They have been discussing a difficult bit of lesson observation feedback that Mona had to give an NQT.

**Krzysztof:**

" *So Mona, tell me more about that.* (Yes, good use of a probe question, helping Mona reflect more deeply...)

**Mona:**

" *Well, for me the hardest thing was the gap between what I observed and her perception of the lesson. I just couldn't think how to close that gap without crushing her...*

**Krzysztof:**

" (That worked well. She's opening up more. Good eye contact, nodding. Wow, I'm on fire here... No hang on, wait a minute, what was she saying? ...) *You see the thing with feedback is striking a balance between positive reinforcement and constructive criticism. The other person needs to feel you are ultimately on her side...* (Damn, now I'm just pontificating and doing all the talking. Ask a question, for goodness sake...) *So, what did you do?*

**Mona:**

" *Well I tried asking her how she thought the lesson went, hoping for some way in, but either she was in denial about what had gone awry, or she genuinely failed to recognise what went wrong.*

**Krzysztof:**

" *So you tried to encourage some self-assessment, but did you try more specific questions to get her thinking about the aspects of her practice that resulted in the lesson becoming a bit chaotic?*

**Mona:**

" *No, I'm not sure I did. What sort of things did you mean?*

**Krzysztof:**

" (Oh damn! That was a closed question, wasn't it? How do I avoid just giving her solutions now?) *Well, let me turn that question back to you Mona. What could you have asked that might have focused her on where she went wrong?* (Woo-hoo! Classic recovery. That was close. Stop talking so much.)

**Mona:**

" *So, like I could have asked how she felt the make-up of the groups affected behaviour and concentration levels later in the lesson?*

**Krzysztof:**

" *I think that's an excellent example. Go on.* (Good, keep her thinking.)

**Mona:**

" *Well I could have asked her how clearly she felt she explained what she wanted from each of the groups, what she did to take account of the different ability levels in the class, and what effect Jamie Clarke's behaviour in particular had on the lesson. But I dunno... I guess I still think the idea that this was a bit of a car crash would leave her in bits.*

**Krzysztof:**

" (Goodness that's a lot of strong language. She looks really tense. Is something else going on here, I wonder?) *How much of this is about your fears, Mona? ...*

## 2. If you only have a hammer

Remember the old adage? Well, if you don't want every mentoring challenge to be a nail, then you need to practise using the full range of question types at your disposal, as well as recognising what sort of questions to avoid.

You may already be familiar with the idea of open and closed questions. Open questions are those which cannot be simply answered yes or no. They often begin with words like where, what, how, when, why, and they invite a fuller answer than closed questions. They are great for encouraging a mentee to talk more and reflect on a topic without imposing any particular agenda or judgement. As a good mentor, you will find yourself using a lot of open questions. For example:

✴ What was successful about that?

✴ Who can you think of who might be helpful here?

✴ When have you felt like this before?

✴ How might you go about doing that?

However, there will be times when a closed question, seeking only a yes or no answer, will be perfectly appropriate – when you are seeking clarification, for example, or ensuring a common understanding.

✴ So, are you saying your dilemma is…?

✴ And you say this needs to be resolved by…?

You may also use closed questions to pin down actions at the end of a conversation.

✴ Are we agreed then that you are going to… by… ?

But what about different sorts of open questions? Hypothetical questions are great for encouraging creativity or shifting perspective.

✴ What would you do if you were feeling at your most confident?

Then there are probing questions and challenging questions.

✴ Why do you think you felt that way?

✴ What are you doing that is preventing you from succeeding here?

There is even something called the 'miracle' or 'magic' question:

✴ Imagine you wake up tomorrow and the problem is solved, what would you notice is different?

Effective mentors use a wide range of questions to provide different sorts of help. However, they are careful to avoid the following:

✴ Multiple questions: *'Why didn't that help, what put you off, and what could you do instead?'*

✴ Leading questions: *'Do you think Trish got upset because you criticised her unfairly?'*

✴ Suggestions disguised as questions: *'What about adopting some sort of merit table?'*

Nira is mentoring Nathan, an experienced colleague who is already regretting agreeing to lead a school-wide literacy initiative. They have begun their conversation by agreeing that Nathan would like some help thinking about how to structure his task and where on earth to start. They have also agreed that this is not something about which Nira is able to offer her own experience. So she is using a variety of questions to help Nathan reflect more deeply:

**Nira:**

" Can you think of a time when you have had to undertake something similar to this? (Effectively a closed question.)

**Nathan:**

" Well nothing really on the literacy front, but I did have to organise a safeguarding inset day at my previous school.

**Nira:**

" OK, and what would you say went well with that? (Open question.)

**Nathan:**

" It all went pretty much to plan as I recall. Apart from just the administration and logistics going smoothly, I actually got a lot of nice comments about how involving the discussions and exercises were. Although, to be honest, I nicked a lot of those ideas from colleagues I'd talked to beforehand!

**Nira:**

" So, what did you do that most contributed to the success of that project, do you think? (Probing open question.)

**Nathan:**

" I'd have to say that the main thing was insisting on a really clear set of aims and objectives for the day. That and planning the hell out of it,

I guess. I remember having a massive chart in my kitchen at home. It was like I was leading the D-Day invasion!

**Nira:**

" It also sounds from what you said earlier, that you had asked for ideas from colleagues. Is that right? (Closed question – checking understanding.)

**Nathan:**

" Yes, I've always been a bit rubbish at the creative thinking thing...

**Nira:**

" Really? What makes you say that? (Open question – challenge.)

**Nathan:**

" Dunno really. I guess I've not really ever regarded myself as the creative type.

**Nira:**

" Well, if you were one of these 'creative types' what lessons would you draw from your safeguarding project experience that you could apply to the literacy initiative? (Hypothetical, open question.)

**A Spot of Theory**

*David Megginson and David Clutterbuck, in their book,* Further Techniques for Coaching and Mentoring *(Butterworth Heinemann, 2009), illustrate a good questioning technique with a list of a hundred 'massively difficult questions'.* Try starting your own collection!

# 3. Let silence be your friend

One of the key skills in being a great listener, and one which we have not yet mentioned, is not talking.

In normal conversation we have a tendency to see silence as the enemy. We feel compelled to fill the shortest pause by saying something, anything. Silence is awkward and uncomfortable, an indication that we are somehow not doing our job of conversing properly. Small wonder then that, as an inexperienced mentor, you may find yourself:

* rapidly following up a great question with another, different question;

* asking a challenging question and then answering it yourself;

* moving the conversation into 'safer' territory;

* firing solutions at your mentee.

All because five seconds have passed without your mentee responding. (Of course, it feels like five minutes.)

So you may need to re-frame your idea of silence. Because, silence also shows you are listening. It slows the conversation down and sends the message that it's fine to just sit and think. It encourages your mentee to reflect more deeply, and, crucially, it gives your mentee the quiet space in which to do this. If you are worried it will all seem too weird, then use your ground rules discussion to talk about how it's okay to sit in silence occasionally, especially when thinking deeply about a difficult topic. It is a necessary part of creating a reflective space.

Two more misconceptions you may need to rid yourself of:

* Demonstrating my skill and helpfulness as a mentor is all about my clever interventions.

* Just listening in silence is too easy and therefore a cop-out.

There is nothing easy about holding on to a silence while attending 100 per cent to your mentee. Sometimes listening, acting as a sounding board and just being there for them is the most helpful thing you can do. Try this four-step approach to exploring a topic.

1. **Question:** Ask a powerful open question.

2. **Tell me more:** Do not simply accept your mentee's initial thinking. Press them to explore more deeply.

3. **Summarise:** Paraphrase back what you think the mentee has been telling you.

4. **Shut up:** Use silence to allow any insight arising from this exchange to surface.

Benjamin is being mentored by Cassie. They work in an inner city primary school which has begun to improve after some years of under-performance and protests from parents. Benjamin is disappointed about being passed over recently for promotion to assistant head, and is discussing his long-term career with his mentor.

**Benjamin:**

" Maybe I should give up on the idea of a leadership position, if I'm so obviously unsuitable. I mean I'm not sure what more I can do than take on projects successfully and consistently get outstanding reports on inspections…

**Cassie:**

" Mmmm, I don't see anyone disputing your talents as an excellent classroom teacher, Benjamin, and I've personally seen you demonstrate leadership, when given the opportunity. So we have to consider what is stopping you being seen as assistant head material. What did you feel you answered well at the interview, and what felt more challenging?

**Benjamin:**

" Well, we talked about the various bits of the school improvement strategy, and I reckon I demonstrated some pretty good contributions in areas like raising physical activity and cracking down on poor classroom behaviour. Maybe I wasn't so strong on after-school club stuff, with me having a bit of a long commute, but that's all…

**Cassie:**

" OK, that's interesting. Say a bit more about that.

**Benjamin:**

" Well, it's a bit like all the work on transition from primary to secondary. Those network meetings with St Luke's High School all took place in the evenings, and I already have to give up time for parents' evenings and stuff.

**Cassie:**

" So I think what I'm hearing is that you can demonstrate a great contribution to the internal aspects of the school improvement plan, but when it comes to the head's key initiative about integrating the school better into the local community and building bridges with parents and partners, you may have less to talk about.

**Benjamin:**

" Oh, I don't know. I've never missed a parents' evening…

**Cassie:**

" (Silence)

**Benjamin:**

" Well, ok, I've not felt able to get as involved in parent–teacher activities as some. I suppose, if I'm honest, I do find the community stuff a bit of a chore… Mmmmm, is it really a key initiative for the head? ….

### A Spot of Theory

In her books, Time to Think and More Time to Think (Fisher King Publishing, 2009), Nancy Kline promotes the value of silence as being where the best ideas often emerge. (It's fair to say it's where your most effective questions sometimes emerge as well!)

# 4. Dig deep

Why are questions so important? They make your mentee *think*. They acknowledge that your mentee has ideas of their own which you value. They help your mentee to plan, analyse and reflect. Most of all, they help your mentee to become more independent and self-reliant. So the quality and depth of your questioning is crucially important.

In both our listening and our questioning as mentors, we can operate at different levels. One of the barriers to progress that mentoring partnerships sometimes encounter is an inability or a reluctance to converse on a more than fairly superficial level. Often, in order to help mentees successfully reflect on experiences or dilemmas which may have occupied their mind for some considerable time before ever talking to you, you need to dig down below the surface facts and behaviour to the beliefs and assumptions which are driving these. You can picture it as an iceberg, where the 'visible' aspects of your mentee's account, the facts, and people's behaviour are the tip of the iceberg, but hidden below the surface are aspects we cannot see, like people's feelings, their values, assumptions and all those things that lie at the root of their behaviour.

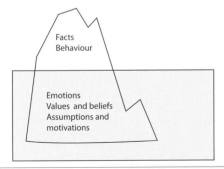

Asking these sorts of questions will probably feel intrusive at first. But if you fail to dig below the surface then you will find yourself trapped in a superficial discussion of technique and behaviours, unable to help your mentee achieve any real insight because neither of you are confronting what motivation lies beneath the challenge they are facing. In other words, your mentee's struggle to manage their work–life balance *may* be all about time management techniques, but it is more likely that it will be at least partly about why they cannot say no to people, or why they set such high standards for themselves, or why they assume any attempt to delegate will fail.

**A Spot of Theory**

*In her book,* Adults Learning *(Open University Press, 2001), Jenny Rogers uses the US Coaches Training Institute model to illustrate the idea of different levels of listening. Level one listeners are still thinking of themselves. They follow their own agenda and give advice. At level two you are focusing on the other person and following their train of thought. At level three you are alert to subtle changes in mood, hearing not just what is said, but also what is being implied or avoided altogether.*

You are mentoring an NQT who wants to improve her behaviour management. Firstly, think of the kind of questions that would constitute the visible section of our 'iceberg'. Jot these down. Now think about what kind of information the answers to these questions might give your mentee.

Then try to formulate some questions that tackle the hidden part of our 'iceberg' – questions that get below the surface of what is happening. Once more, try to imagine what the answers to these questions might tell your mentee.

Once you have done this, compare your thoughts with the examples below.

## 'Surface' questions

* *Can you give me a recent example of when you felt you failed to manage behaviour as well as you would like? What happened?*

* *Can you give me a recent example of when you felt you managed behaviour really well? What happened?*

* *Tell me what happens when you feel behaviour in the classroom is getting out of control.*

* *What behaviour management strategies have you tried? How well have these worked for you?*

* *Who do you regard as being really good at this? What do they do?*

## 'Deeper' questions

* *What constitutes good behaviour for you?*

* *What kind of relationship are you hoping for with learners?*

* *How do you feel when behaviour deteriorates? What response does this trigger in you?*

* *What are you assuming about your learners and what they want?*

* *What assumptions are driving your own behaviour?*

You can see that 'surface' questions will provide useful information about examples and specific challenges, but what 'deeper' questions provide is a better understanding of expectations and key 'triggers'. Only these sorts of questions will help your mentee to understand, for example, that it may be their desire to be popular, rather than ignorance of technique, that is preventing them from keeping order adequately.

*So, Craig, tell me how you feel about that?*

Use this to keep a record of what worked well for you and what didn't. Not every strategy will suit every school, or perhaps be practicable. There's a line at the bottom for you to add your own strategy, if it's not already included.

| Strategy | Tried it with… | On…(date) | It worked | It didn't work | Worth trying again? |
|---|---|---|---|---|---|
| 1. Watch yourself<br>   A. Talking ratio<br>   B. Questions versus statements<br>   C. Open to closed | | | | | |
| 2. If you only have a hammer | | | | | |
| **3. Let silence be your friend*** | | | | | |
| 4. Dig deep | | | | | |
| Your own strategy? | | | | | |

# DAY 5: Helping your mentee develop further

Now it is time to broaden your repertoire of skills and techniques by delving a little deeper into the mentor's toolkit. As your principal aim in all this is to generate insight, it is worth considering how this works and what kind of things get in the way.

One way to gain insight is by making **connections**. You realise that a situation you are encountering in the classroom is actually very similar to something else you have experienced. Or, alternatively, you begin to understand how something you do or say has triggered an unexpected behaviour in your learners or a colleague. Maybe, on reflection, you recognise how a particularly successful lesson was the result of meticulous preparation or complete spontaneity. We know that our brains are hard-wired to make these connections and that we tend to find the process energising, so this is one way in which your mentoring technique can be helpful to your mentee.

The opposite side of this coin is that you can also achieve insight from **contradictions**. So, as a mentor, you should find ways of helping your mentee identify things that do *not* fit their current narrative. You might get them to think of times when they have felt more or less positive, successful, confident, anxious, etc. Remember what we covered in the previous chapter about *depth* of questioning and listening? You are trying to put your mentee in touch with the perspectives, attitudes and assumptions that are influencing how they act. This is because we know that even small changes in these assumptions can bring about large changes in behaviour and state of mind.

So what gets in the way of insight? Self-awareness can be blocked by those defence mechanisms that we all throw up occasionally. These might include denial (a sometimes aggressive refusal to accept the connections or contradictions in front of us), repression (not allowing our real feelings to surface), rationalisation or intellectualisation (hiding behind manufactured reasons or excuses for events), and, even more commonly perhaps, humour (trying to side-step the truth by engaging our mentor in a joke).

## Today's strategies

1. Mirror, mirror

2. Look at it this way

3. I wanna tell you a story

4. Thanks for sharing

*Can you think of a time when you have felt more positive, confident, inspired?*

# 1. Mirror, mirror

There are a number of ways that you can act as a mirror to your mentee, helping them to see themselves in a different light. First of all, you can try **summarising and reflecting back**. This means listening attentively to what your mentee is telling you and then paraphrasing this back to them *along with some added value of your own*. This 'added value' is not about you putting words into your mentee's mouth, nor is it about imposing your own interpretation on events. It merely means noticing something about the mentee's language, demeanour or previous experiences which you think might be connected to (or contradicting) what they are saying.

What you are offering your mentee here is a form of **feedback**, and there are a number of other ways you can use feedback to hold up a mirror to your mentee.

You can help your mentee to think about the **sources of feedback** available to them. Apart from you, where might they look to get a view of themselves as others see them? Classroom observations, obviously, but also co-teaching, appraisal, learner feedback, family, friends... The list could be a long one. Once they have sought out appropriate feedback, you are in a privileged position, as their mentor, to help them process and make sense of it.

Next, you might offer the mentoring session as a safe space in which your mentee can **rehearse** some activity, such as a tricky conversation with a learner/colleague or a meeting with their head of department. This will allow you to give direct feedback on what you observe.

Alternatively, you can rely on **your own experience of the mentee**. You have spent many hours talking together. What do you observe them doing and what impact does this have on you?

Finally, there is what mentors call *'feedback in the moment'*. This is when you are discussing something with your mentee and you notice something: a sudden shift in mood or facial expression, a hesitation, a sigh or a change in style of language. Noticing this and immediately feeding back to your mentee what you observe can highlight a connection or contradiction that leads to deeper insight.

*As we start to discuss feedback, I notice you show some signs of anxiety.*

Let us take a look at some of these ways of holding up a mirror to your mentee. What might they sound like? Read each example and see if you can identify which of the following three techniques they best resemble.

A.   summarising and reflecting back;

B.   your own experience of the mentee;

C.   feedback in the moment.

## Example 1

*Can I just share an observation with you here, Wesley? You are telling me that you're willing to work with some of your younger colleagues to bring these aspects of your subject knowledge more up to date. But I notice, even as we agree this, that you are avoiding eye contact and looking pretty cheesed off. How committed to his strategy are you really?*

## Example 2

*OK, Nadiya, what you are telling me is that you feel as though you ought to go for the head of department role, because you've got the experience and skills, and people are going to expect you to progress into a leadership role by this stage in your career. I also hear you talking about how much you love your current job, what a kick you get out of working with the A level students. But I'm just not sensing the same energy and enthusiasm when you talk about a management role, and there's a bit of fear and trepidation in your description of this.*

## Example 3

*You are clearly finding working with Howard on the literacy project a real struggle. You're very different people, and I absolutely see how some of his behaviour might rub you up the wrong way. I'm sure it's been frustrating for both of you. The only thing we can usefully talk about in these sessions, however, is you. I wonder if it would be helpful if I just shared with you some helpful feedback about how you come across to me, and see if that triggers any thoughts about how adjusting your approach might make things easier with Howard?*

### A Spot of Theory

*In her book,* Coaching Skills *(Open University Press, 2004), Jenny Rogers has some helpful guidelines for how, as a mentor, you might role model for your mentee the right way to handle feedback:*

● don't get angry/offended;

● don't confess 'guilt';

● repeat and summarise back;

● ask for evidence;

● ask for ideas on improvement;

● give your side if necessary.

## 2. Look at it this way

Another way that your mentee can achieve greater insight is to re-frame events, experiences and challenges so as to see them in a different light. There are a number of different approaches you might take to help them with this.

Try encouraging your mentee to look at things from a different **perspective**. (This is particularly useful if they are struggling with communication or relationships in some way.) As a default position, most of us tend to look at what is happening from our own point of view only. So try asking your mentee what the following 'people' are thinking or feeling:

- the other person(s) involved in the scenario being discussed;
- an entirely disinterested (and imaginary) outside observer;
- the school or college, as personified by the head or chair of governors.

A more sophisticated version of this technique is actually to ask your mentee to role play another perspective while you voice *their* take on things.

Of particular relevance when using contradictions as a route to insight is searching for **exceptions**. You can use this to challenge what are known as 'self-limiting beliefs', when your mentee convinces herself that she is hopeless at some activity or other. Simply ask if she can remember a time when she engaged in this activity successfully. What was different about that occasion? If your mentee is facing a challenging situation with trepidation, then ask him if he has faced a similar situation before and triumphed.

In order to re-frame things, mentees sometimes need to let go of a particular cognitive loop they have got themselves stuck in, whether that be paralysis over a decision or a deep-seated habit they find hard to break. You can use **'catastrophising'**, asking them what the worst possible consequence of a particular decision or action might be. (It's generally less severe than they are assuming.) Or alternatively you could use **exaggeration**. Take a particular behaviour and ask your mentee to imagine what the result of taking this to the extreme might look and feel like.

**A Spot of Theory**

*In their book,* Techniques for Coaching and Mentoring *(Butterworth Heinemann, 2005), David Megginson and David Clutterbuck outline a tool called 'Separate selves', where a mentor asks their mentee to identify conflicts between, say, their active and their passive self or their optimistic and pessimistic self, or their private and public self.*

Take a look at the scenario outlined below. Then have a go at jotting down how you could help shift the mentee's view of events using each of the three techniques described below:

A.   perspectives;

B.   exceptions;

C.   catastrophising or exaggerating.

You teach in the languages department of a large secondary school or FE college and you are mentoring Mel, a colleague in the science department who is anxious about her forthcoming appraisal with her boss, Simon. The two of them have clashed quite publicly over aspects of the new marking and assessment regime the head of department has introduced, and Mel has become convinced that Simon *'has it in for her'* on the basis of a couple of projects he has given her which she thinks are designed to make her fail, so he can formally criticise her performance.

You don't know Simon well, but suspect his motives may not be as sinister as Mel seems to think, given some of the nice things you have heard about Simon's reputation as a manager from other colleagues.

What questions might you ask, using each of these three techniques, for shifting a mentee's view? Once you have jotted these down, compare your thoughts with the examples given below:

A.   **Perspectives**

*What is it that Simon needs from you Mel? What do you see as the main challenges that he has? What has Simon to gain from you messing up this project?*

B.   **Exceptions**

*Can you think of instances when Simon has praised your work? Which boss have you had the best relationship with? How was your behaviour different with them, compared to when you were with Simon?*

C.   **Catastrophising or exaggerating**

*If you shared your misgivings with Simon about the way your relationship has developed, what do think is the worst that might happen? What do you think the best outcome might be? Assuming your very worst fears about Simon's intentions are true, describe how you see this appraisal panning out. What if we assume the very best intentions on his part? What then? Which of these outcomes seems most realistic, do you think?*

# 3. I wanna tell you a story

Ever noticed how sometimes insights can spring from the most unexpected associations? You'll be reading a book or watching your favourite television programme, and it will trigger a new thought about an issue that you hadn't even been consciously thinking about. Reflection and creative ideas can often flourish best when our minds are allowed to wander.

One way of stimulating this kind of reflection is storytelling. Not only do stories allow our minds to wander, they also help to:

* depersonalise and 'distance' ourselves from what might be a sensitive or risky topic;

* free us from the limitations of 'real life';

* embody different perspectives and motivations in each protagonist.

So you might ask your mentee if a situation reminds them of a particular story, and which character they would most associate themselves (and others) with. How would he see the story unfolding, if he were the author? You might ask her to recount a particular experience as though it were a fairy story or crime thriller. The real benefit comes from how you follow this up with questions about how the mentee has chosen to frame the experience and allocate characters.

If this feels a bit 'over the top', try starting with individual metaphors. For example, if you notice your mentee using imagery around gambling (throw the dice, trust to luck, I'll bet you...), or warfare (it's indefensible, I felt under attack, she shot me down), then stop and explore this further. Who is the enemy? What is at stake? What are the odds? Is there a peace plan?

You do not have to fictionalise events. You could choose to encourage deeper insight by asking your mentee to recount real-life stories about themselves. Of course, you lose the protection afforded by distancing and depersonalising events, but you may both learn more about the mentee's beliefs, passions and fears. The essential thing here is to be specific and focus on a critical incident.

* *Tell me about a time when you have felt most fulfilled.*

* *Tell me about when you have felt most demotivated.*

* *Tell me about a particularly stimulating challenge.*

---

You are listening attentively as your mentee, Riya, recounts her experiences, or 'story' in the run-up to a potentially difficult transition from Reception classteacher in your village primary school to taking over Year 2. She is clearly not looking forward to the change! Read through this account, imagining you are hearing this as a mentor, and see how many clues or opportunities you can spot for further exploration. For each one, think about what kind of question you might like to ask.

## Riya's story

*This has been my fifth year taking the Reception class, and I just love it. There's something about kids at that age, when they can still learn so much from playing, that feels so untainted by the cynicism that can creep into the school environment. You don't feel so caged in by the curriculum and the tests and the standards. I sometimes think it's like a different little world where the joy of discovery and the wonder at new things hasn't yet been beaten out of the poor little mites by the demands of Her Majesty's stormtroopers and their key stages! I worry that it will be like I'm going from being the BFG, helping these littlies discover new treasures every day, to being Miss Trunchbull, cramming the national curriculum into kids' heads like they were jam doughnuts. And the parents, what about them? It's bad enough in Reception, when they're virtually trying to follow little Jimmy into the classroom because they're almost as traumatised by the thought of separation as he is. But at least they're mainly focused on the kids' happiness. What's it going to be like when I'm in the firing line for the performance of their little darlings in Key Stage 1, and all these aspirational parents are battling for their offspring to be not just on target, but better than all the rest? I mean, I know in my head that this is a good move for me, experience-wise, and I'm sure I can get my head down and battle through all these feelings eventually, but in my heart I know I'll miss what I'm leaving behind...*

**A Spot of Theory**

*In his book,* The Stories We Live By *(Guilford Press, 1993), Dan McAdams suggests some other types of story you can ask about as well.*

- **Turning point:** A time in your career when you had to undergo substantial change.
- **Stress experience:** A time when you experienced a lot of negative pressure in your work.

# 4. Thanks for sharing

It may have dawned on you, reading these last two chapters, that as you try to help your mentee learn from new insights, you will find yourself moving up and down a continuum of directiveness. Remember this aspect of mentoring from Day 1?

So you may only have to do something relatively non-directive, such as ask a powerful question, reflect back an observation, or even just sit and listen, in order for that metaphorical light bulb to come on above your mentee's head. Or it may be that you have to resort to more directive interventions, such as offering your mentee some challenging feedback. As a skilled mentor, you will judge where to position your approach along this spectrum on the basis of two factors:

* your mentee's experience and expertise around the issue under discussion (less experienced or competent mentees may require more directive interventions);

* the general rule of thumb that non-directive approaches result in better quality learning and should therefore be tried first.

What is the justification for this last observation? Well, by and large the more directive we become with our mentee the less we:

* allow him to **think for himself**;

* engender **self-motivation** and fun;

* enable her to know **how** she got a result;

* allow her to use her own **language and experiences**;

* help him **remember** what he's learned.

So it would be disastrous to give mentors carte blanche to bang on about their own experiences and strategies, particularly when their mentee might actually have a better idea. An overuse of 'do what I do' in mentoring in schools can lead to the ossification of the status quo and the stifling of real innovation.

That said, there will clearly be times when it is legitimate to share your own experiences with your mentee, as another way of provoking greater insight, provided that you realise the potential pitfalls of what is quite a directive technique. Skilled mentors will be able to recognise when this is appropriate. They will also be able to do it in such a way as to avoid imposing solutions on the mentee and to leave responsibility with them as to how they use any new insight.

So how do you share your own experiences and expertise in a way that is compatible with effective mentoring? Well, first of all, you avoid imposing your own ideas by asking *permission*, or *offering*, to share some experience. It might sound something like this:

" *Actually, Jamil, I've been faced with this kind of dilemma myself when discovering what I've thought may be plagiarism. Would it be helpful at all for me to say a bit about my experience?*

Secondly, always be *transparent* about offering alternatives. Don't disguise these as 'fake' questions, like *'Have you thought of...?'* Simply say:

" *There is another option, Karen, that I don't think you've mentioned, which is...*

Thirdly, if possible always try to offer your mentee some *choice*. This avoids the implication that there is only one correct answer and it happens to be the one you chose! So you might choose to phrase things like this:

" *When I, or other colleagues, have been faced with having to confront a parent about this kind of thing, there are a couple of different approaches that have proved quite effective...*

The important thing here is, having shared some experience, to stop and leave the mentee to draw their own conclusions. For some reason, having adopted a more directive style, it is very easy to get stuck in that mode, and simply keep firing off suggestions. For this reason, you may find the discipline of forcing yourself back into questioning helps. So try finishing with:

" *What do you make of what we've discussed? What further thoughts has that generated about the topic? What course of action does all of that suggest to you?*

The important thing here is to try and ensure that the mentee retains the responsibility for their own solution and whatever action arises from their insights.

**A Spot of Theory**

*If you wish to explore this issue further, the approach described above is taken from Myles Downey's book,* Effective Coaching *(Texere, 2003).*

**Checklist**

Use this to keep a record
of what worked well for
you and what didn't. Not
every strategy will suit
every school, or perhaps
be practicable. There's a
line at the bottom for you
to add your own strategy, if
it's not already included.

| Strategy | Tried it with... | On...(date) | It worked | It didn't work | Worth trying again? |
|---|---|---|---|---|---|
| 1. Mirror, mirror | | | | | |
| A. Summarising and reflecting back | | | | | |
| B. Rehearsal | | | | | |
| C. Sources of feedback | | | | | |
| D. Your own experience of the mentee | | | | | |
| E. Feedback in the moment | | | | | |
| **2. Look at it this way*** | | | | | |
| A. Perspectives | | | | | |
| B. Exceptions | | | | | |
| C. Catastrophising or exaggerating | | | | | |
| 3. I wanna tell you a story | | | | | |
| 4. Thanks for sharing | | | | | |
| Your own strategy? | | | | | |

# DAY 6: Common challenges

You have spent a couple of days studying some of the skills and techniques you need to be a great mentor. Now it is time to look at how you might combine these skills and apply them to some of the more common challenges with which you might be confronted. These are concerned with helping your mentee to:

* identify a compelling purpose for the mentoring partnership. What do they want to gain from it and why is this important to them?;

* improve their self-awareness. Is a lack of clear-sightedness about their strengths, behaviour or impact on others holding them back?;

* cope better with adversity. How well are they managing the stresses and demands of the job?;

* maintain productive relationships with others. Are unnecessary conflicts, rivalries or resentments getting in the way?;

* achieve sustainable changes in behaviour. How do you successfully adopt and maintain new practices and behaviours?

As a general rule, most of the strategies you are about to learn fall into one of two broad categories. Sometimes you can help your mentee most effectively by concentrating their attention on the wider context, or **'panning out'** from the topic under discussion. On other occasions, it may seem more useful to delve deeper into detailed examples, or **'zoom in'**. A typical 'panning out' kind of question would be:

> " *What is it you really want to achieve here?*

Alternatively, a 'zooming in' question might be something like:

> " *Can you think of a specific incident that illustrates this? Tell me what happened.*

You may even find yourself moving between these two approaches as you jointly wrestle with a particular problem or dilemma. One helpful way of ensuring that your mentee is prepared to engage in this kind of reflection is to suggest they keep some sort of brief log of events between mentoring conversations, recording instances of particular successes or frustrations.

## Today's strategies

1. Why am I here? Building purpose

2. Who am I? Building self-awareness

3. What have I done to deserve this? Building resilience

4. Who does she think she is? Building relationships

5. How will I keep this up? Building new habits

---

# 1. Why am I here? Building purpose

A common reason mentoring partnerships stagnate and fail to achieve their potential is that insufficient attention is paid early on to what the mentoring is intended to achieve. There is some debate in the current literature as to whether detailed goals and objectives are always helpful in mentoring, or whether they can sometimes be counter-productive. However, most commentators would agree that an overall sense of purpose at least is essential to ensuring that mentoring conversations are productive and engaging and not just a series of cosy chats.

A. **Visioning:** One way of identifying purpose is to use **visioning**. Ask your mentee to describe in some detail what a perfect career move, school environment, line manager, lesson or school day would look and feel like. The answer will undoubtedly be a mixture of reality and fantasy, but it might well point you both towards a fruitful focus for your conversations. A variation on this idea is to start by getting all your mentee's anxieties and frustrations out by asking questions like:

* What is keeping you awake at night?
* What is holding you back at work?
* What would you most like to change about your job?

Following this, use visioning to explore what would be different in their 'perfect world'.

B. **Challenges:** Another approach is to work from **challenges.** Ask your mentee what key challenges will be facing them over, say, the next couple of years, and then explore what new and different skills, knowledge or behaviours they might need to face these challenges. You can even pan out further by starting with what challenges the school or college is facing, and then moving on to how this impacts on them.

C. **Connections and contradictions:** Or, you could turn to these two key catalysts of insight that we looked at in the last chapter. Get your mentee talking generally about their current job, what brought them to where they are, and their hopes and dreams for the future. As they tell their story, listen out for aspects that seem to fit well together and things that appear contradictory or in conflict. Use summary and reflecting back to 'replay' this to your mentee. If you have understood correctly, does this indicate any useful areas of focus for the mentoring?

**A Spot of Theory**

*For a thought-provoking examination of the evidence for and against detailed goal-setting in mentoring and coaching, try reading* Beyond Goals: Effective Strategies for Coaching and Mentoring *(Gower, 2013) by Susan David, David Clutterbuck and David Megginson.*

You are mentoring an experienced colleague who has recently moved to your school. You have had a couple of conversations but find yourselves **struggling to identify the best focus for your discussions**. He comes to your sessions with his head full of random thoughts and anxieties about his job, but seems incapable of distinguishing what really matters and how his own skills and behaviour might relate to this.

**What approaches might you employ here and what sort of questions would you ask in order to help him think more clearly about what he wants the mentoring to do for him?**

You may find it useful to consider first what might be causing this difficulty.

Once you have had a think and jotted a few things down, take a look at some of the suggestions below.

It could be that your mentee has simply not given enough thought to what they want and needs help finding some focus for their development. In this case, helpful questions might include:

- *What do you reckon the most challenging aspects of the school strategy are going to be over the next couple of years? How might you best contribute to this as a new member of staff?*

- *What is going to be the most difficult thing about your new role here do you think?*

- *What are the skills/behaviours you're going to need more of in order to respond to this?*

- *If you look back on this job in a couple of years' time, what will make the difference between it having been an 'OK' two years and a fantastic two years?*

- *What do you need to do to ensure it's a fantastic two years?*

On the other hand, it may be that your mentee is reluctant to admit to needing help this soon into a new post. In this case your questions might be different.

- *What are the main differences you notice between your previous school and here?*

- *How do you feel about these? What do you think we could learn? What might you learn from us?*

- *Let's talk about some of the best and worst things about changing schools from our own experience. Shall I start?*

## 2. Who am I? Building self-awareness

An effective approach for thinking about personal and professional development is to focus on **core qualities**. First ask your mentee to think about what they are great at and what their toughest challenges have been. Help them to think about feedback they have received, achievements they are proud of and challenges they have met successfully, as well as times they have been less successful. You may need to challenge blind spots or self-limiting beliefs by seeking exceptions or pressing them for specific evidence and examples. See if this generates some thoughts about what they regard as their core qualities. The next step is to ask your mentee to talk about what happens when they demonstrate *too much* of their core qualities.

This uses a concept devised by Toby Rhodes known as *'overstrengths'*. It works from the assumption that the aspects of our skills and behaviour that can be most destructive and unsuccessful are actually closely related to our positive qualities, rather than the polar opposite. For example, your mentee might be fantastic at planning lessons, but then struggle with responding spontaneously to unplanned events or setbacks. Alternatively, she may have an easy and informal rapport with students, but occasionally avoid tough decisions for fear of being disliked. The overstrengths idea will get you talking about behaviours as well as just skills.

Remember the 'Knowing me, knowing you' strategies in the Day 3 chapter? Try returning to the values and beliefs to which your mentee subscribes, and asking them how this affects such things as:

* the sort of behaviour that provokes a negative reaction in them;

* the aspects of their behaviour that may trigger a negative reaction in others.

By mapping your mentee's responses onto the core quadrants model designed by Daniel Ofman (1992, 2001), you can summarise these thoughts on a grid like the one below. This will enable your mentee to look at themselves from a variety of perspectives, rather than getting stuck in a simplistic analysis of strengths and weaknesses. The idea here is that the most realistic development goals for your mentee will involve comparison between the top left quadrant and the bottom right.

| CORE QUALITY (What key strengths most define you? Eg A BORN PLANNER, ORGANISED) | PITFALL (What happens when your core quality goes too far? Eg RIGID, INFLEXIBLE) |
|---|---|
| ALLERGY (What do you hate most in others? Eg LAISSEZ-FAIRE, MESSINESS, UNPREDICTABILITY) | CHALLENGE (What do you lack, and wish you had more of? Eg ADAPTABILITY, SPONTANEITY) |

*Would you consider this an overstrength or an under stress Jill?*

Let's listen in on a conversation between Josh and his mentee, Nathan, who is struggling to get lesson preparation and marking done on time, without spending a much greater proportion of his weekend on it than he would like...

**Nathan:**

66 *I know everyone moans about the workload, but I'm working all day Sunday and if I duck out of another cricket match I'm going to get dropped from the team for good.*

**Josh:**

66 *Has this always been a challenge for you then, Nathan?*

**Nathan:**

66 *Well, yeah, kind of, but I suppose it's got worse as I've taken on more advanced students and different topics. Don't get me wrong, I like being busy...*

**Josh:**

66 *Describe busy for me.*

**Nathan:**

66 *Oh, you know, I love having lots of stuff on the go at the same time, lots of balls in the air... Keeps me energised, all that running around. I love the variety, the next thing to sort out...*

**Josh:**

66 *So, if I were to ask people close to you what core quality of yours that demonstrated, what would they say?*

**Nathan:**

66 *Energy, I guess, enthusiasm, the ability to keep lots of things in my head at once without dropping the ball, as it were... I get really frustrated with people who just plod along one thing at a time, and can't break off for one second to answer a question or deal with an immediate issue.*

**Josh:**

66 *Brilliant, yes, I think I would recognise that. It's some of the things that make you fun to work with. But what are some of the consequences of this quality if you push it too far?*

**Nathan:**

66 *I suppose I'm better at starting stuff than finishing it, so sometimes something important slips through the net 'cos I'm really enjoying sorting out the lab equipment or putting a cool chart together for the wall...*

**Josh:**

66 *So how could you set about bringing a bit more prioritisation and sustained focus into how you work, without losing all that enthusiasm and energy?*

***If you were to draw Nathan's core qualities matrix, what would it look like?***

**A Spot of Theory**

*Self-awareness is the cornerstone of emotional intelligence. Only by understanding our own impact on others can we develop the ability to handle our emotions appropriately, recognise feelings in others, and manage conflict and collaboration more effectively. See more in Daniel Goleman's book,* Emotional Intelligence *(Bloomsbury, 1996).*

# 3. What have I done to deserve this? Building resilience

We can define resilience as our ability to respond constructively to both normal job demands and setbacks. Faced with a mentee who is struggling to do this, you may need first to help them develop greater self-awareness, using the kind of approaches already outlined. Here are some other more specific strategies.

A.  Knowing what is most important to us gives us an insight into what our particular **'stress triggers'** might be. According to research, some of the things that unsettle people to different degrees are:

- lack of control or autonomy;
- absence of strong relationships;
- dissatisfaction with ourselves;
- uncertainty;
- lack of development/growth opportunities;
- unclear purpose;
- injustice/unfairness.

B.  Ask about their **'typical' response to events**. Are they naturally inclined to be optimistic about the future, or are they more of a 'glass half-empty' sort of a person? How secure is their self-esteem? How naturally persistent are they? Understanding such aspects of our personality, aspects which are unlikely to change radically, provides important clues to how we deal with adversity and what we can and cannot do to get better at it.

C.  Try helping your mentee to identify what kind of things most **drain their resilience** and what **restores their sense of well-being**. Ask them what they could do to tip the balance more towards well-being.

Your mentee's response to job demands and adverse events will also be determined by their automatic assumptions about such things as:

- their own capabilities;
- how much control they have;
- other people's motives;
- what others want from them;
- how success will be measured, etc.

You may be able to help them make more helpful or more accurate assumptions, which will, in turn, affect their response to events.

For example, your mentee may be feeling overwhelmed by a build-up of challenges, many of which he has no direct control over. Exploring these assumptions and helping him differentiate between what he can and cannot control, will help him focus his energies on what he can change, stop worrying about what he cannot, and hopefully restore his sense of self-efficacy.

You are mentoring a colleague who moved to your FE college from a small secondary school about 12 months ago. You have made progress in building positive rapport, and helping her adapt to a different culture. However, it is clear that the job is still frequently getting her down. She complains of 'stress' and you have noticed the difficulty she has bouncing back when things don't go as well as she would like. This is not like her, and you wonder what's going on.

- ✦ What approaches might you employ here to try and help her improve her resilience to the normal demands of the job?
- ✦ What kind of questions would you ask in such circumstances?

Given that this is something new for your mentee, you might begin by asking a general question about what has been going on in her life. She talks about having finally sold her house and relocated from Yorkshire. This is much better for work, but means she is further away from her 90-year-old mother, and feels guilty about visiting less.

You ask what else is a drain on her resilience at the moment, and she talks about missing her colleagues at her old school, particularly the way they supported each other and provided reassurance whenever any of them worried about their ability to cope with the job. You reflect back that she has talked before about her lack of self-confidence and uncertainty over her performance in the new job. You wonder aloud what used to bolster her resilience in the past.

In addition to a close network of friends, both in school and out of it, she cites her previous boss as a great one for giving regular feedback. In a bigger institution, she now feels a bit left to drift, and unsure if what she is doing is appreciated or valued.

You summarise some of this for her, and ask what she could do to stay in touch with old friends more effectively, and maybe build another network in her new location.

You also agree that, before the next session she will have a think about what she could do to elicit more feedback, both formal and informal.

### A Spot of Theory

*In his book,* The 7 Habits of Highly Effective People *(Rosetta Books, 1989), Steven Covey explains how our 'circle of concern' (what we worry about) is always bigger than our 'circle of influence' (what we can truly control). Try helping your mentee map their worries against these two concentric circles.*

# 4. Who does she think she is? Building relationships

We all struggle to build and maintain productive relationships at some point in our working lives, whether that is with colleagues, students, parents or our school leaders. As you will have already seen earlier in this chapter, self-awareness is the keystone to managing relationships more effectively. So, many of the strategies we have already covered may well be useful to you when faced with this particular challenge. However, here are some further ideas.

A.  **Using needs as a way of exploring conflict and collaboration:** You can help your mentee discount some of the emotional 'baggage' and personality factors in a tricky relationship by getting them to consider mutual needs. First ask her to identify what exactly she needs from the other person. You may need to be quite challenging here in order to keep her focused on functional outcomes, rather than *'I need him to be less of an idiot'*. Help her prioritise. What is really important?

Then invite your mentee to put themselves in the other person's shoes. What does she think *he* needs? Really encourage her to try and get inside the other person's head. This alone will help to build greater understanding and empathy. Having produced these two lists, you can ask your mentee a number of further questions.

* *How reasonable are your needs/his needs?*
* *What does this tell you about possible sources of conflict?*
* *Do you see any opportunities here for cooperation, mutual help or learning?*
* *What are you able to change that will make this relationship work better?*

B.  An extended version of this idea is a hypothetical version of what is called **'role negotiation'**. You ask your mentee to imagine a structured dialogue with their colleague/boss/team member/etc in which they each share their answers to the following three questions.

* *What are two things I value about you and would like you to keep doing?*
* *What are two things I would like you to do more of?*
* *What are two things I find unhelpful and would like you to do less/ stop doing?*

What does this suggest about possible ways of improving the working relationship?

**A Spot of Theory**

*The idea of 'role negotiation' was developed by Roger Harrison, an organisation development thinker, who suggested it as a way of improving teamwork. You can read more about this in the book,* Collected Papers of Roger Harrison *(McGraw-Hill, 1995).*

At this point, let's go back to Josh and Nathan. As we have seen, they have had some useful discussions about core qualities. However, they are now getting a bit bogged down in the problems Nathan is having with a particular colleague, Deidre, which he despairingly puts down to his *'inability to suffer fools gladly'*.

**Josh:**

" That's quite strong language, Nathan. What is it exactly that makes Deidre a 'fool'?

**Nathan:**

" Oh blimey, have you seen her? She has one speed, which is dead slow, and she plods along with whatever she's doing like a mule. I completely lost it with her the other day, because I just needed her to cover my break duty for ten minutes while I quickly sorted out these two or three things with a lab experiment and next week's rugby fixture, and something else that I've now forgotten, and blow me if she didn't simply refuse because she hadn't quite finished marking a bloody assignment!

**Josh:**

" How often has this sort of thing happened before?

**Nathan:**

" Oh, two or three times at least. But it won't happen again, because she's not even talking to me now…

**Josh:**

" You remember we talked about core qualities before, and you identified what your 'allergy' quadrant might contain. This behaviour of Deidre's that you've described sounds like it might fit right in there.

**Nathan:**

" Yes, I suppose it does, but that doesn't make it right.

**Josh:**

" What if we stop thinking about this in terms of right or wrong, Nathan, and focus on what you could do to enable you both to work more harmoniously together? For example, how do you think Deidre sees you?

**Nathan:**

" Before she stopped talking to me, she called me a disorganised dilettante dragging a trail of broken commitments.

**Josh:**

" Well, her insults have more class than yours, at least! What do you suppose she would like more of from you?

**Nathan:**

" Sudden changes obviously freak her out a bit, so I guess she would like me to give her more notice of needing help, and show that I'm only doing that in the case of real priorities…

# 5. How will I keep this up? Building new habits

Change is difficult. If you've ever tried to take more exercise, or diet, or give up smoking, or any other significant change in behaviour like this, then you will appreciate that making the change and sticking to it is not easy.

As a mentor, part of your role, and one of your greatest challenges, is to help your mentee try new behaviours, acquire new skills and strategies and apply these with a degree of consistency. In doing so, there are three key factors that can make the process a lot easier, or a lot harder for your mentee:

- ✸ a real sense of *need*;
- ✸ *agency* – a feeling of being in control and capable of change;
- ✸ a *routemap* – having the change broken down into manageable steps.

## Need

Ask your mentee why the change is important. What does it mean to them? Sometimes people agree to take a particular action because they feel they should, or they want to please you, or they are finding the conversation awkward. If they do not feel a real need to change, your mentee will fall at the first hurdle. Try discussing pay-offs and benefits. Use visioning. In what ways will things be easier/happier/more satisfying if they succeed in this change? What might the negative consequences of no change be?

## Agency

Assuming your mentee can articulate a strong sense of need, how confident is he of adopting this new strategy or behaviour? Does he feel this is within his capabilities? How confident does he feel of success? Why is this? Is there a need for more explanation, support or rehearsal in order for him to take the plunge? What is holding him back?

## Routemap

Finally, even if your mentee has a compelling need to try this, and feels confident they can do it, it might all fall apart if the scale of the task is just too much to tackle head-on. Ask your mentee questions such as *'What would be the easiest place to start?'* or *'How could we break this down into smaller steps?'* or *'What would feel comfortable to you as an initial goal?'*

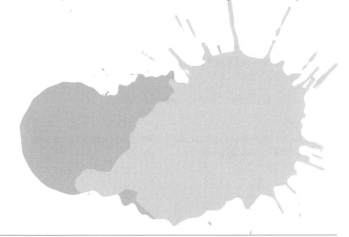

You and a student teacher have enjoyed a productive session looking at ways of improving classroom behaviour by adopting different strategies for different 'personalities' in the class. As you try to identify an action plan, however, she starts to be a little evasive, claiming it's all a bit daunting. You've noted that her past record on completing agreed actions is poor.

How might you use the strategy above to help her identify actions that really motivate her and ratchet up her commitment to getting something constructive done about the issue?

You might begin, then, by evaluating her sense of *need*. How convinced is she that improving classroom management will improve her lessons, or is she more concerned that imposing additional discipline might stifle creativity or undermine her rapport with students? You would want to ask questions like:

- *If you were able to better control some of the disruptive elements in the class, what would the benefits be for the other students and you personally? What might be the downsides?*

- *Tell me about the most satisfying and successful lesson you've run recently and the least. What part did behaviour management play in these results?*

Moving on to your mentee's feelings of *agency*, to what extent does she feel capable of experimenting with new behaviour management practices? Is she agreeing in order to please you, without feeling confident that she can change her approach? Is she scared of how some students might respond? So you ask...

- *Let's imagine you are delivering tomorrow's lesson and the usual suspects are 'kicking off', how confident do you feel about responding as we discussed, on a scale of one to ten?*

- *What would need to be different for you to score this higher?*

Finally, perhaps you have concluded that *need* and *agency* are not the problem here. What if this is simply a case of not knowing where to start? How do you ensure that your mentee is 'eating the elephant' in small enough chunks? Well, you might ask:

- *Which of the strategies we've discussed today do you reckon would be easiest for you to try? Why don't we start there?*

- *If we were to look at making these changes over, say, a whole term, how would you choose to 'phase them in'?*

Use this to keep a record of what worked well for you and what didn't. Not every strategy will suit every school, or perhaps be practicable. There's a line at the bottom for you to add your own strategy, if it's not already included.

| Strategy | Tried it with... | On...(date) | It worked | It didn't work | Worth trying again? |
|---|---|---|---|---|---|
| 1. Why am I here? Building purpose | | | | | |
| A. Visioning | | | | | |
| B. Challenges | | | | | |
| C. Connections and contradictions | | | | | |
| **2. Who am I? Building self-awareness*** | | | | | |
| 3. What have I done to deserve this? – Building resilience | | | | | |
| A. Stress triggers | | | | | |
| B. Typical response | | | | | |
| C. Draining and restoring | | | | | |
| 4. Who does she think she is? Building relationships | | | | | |
| A. Using needs as a way of exploring conflict and collaboration | | | | | |
| B. Role negotiation | | | | | |
| 5. How will I keep this up? Building new habits | | | | | |
| Your own strategy? | | | | | |

# DAY 7: Is it working? Evaluating success

Welcome to Day 7, the final day in this book, but hopefully just the start of your mentoring journey. It seems appropriate today to consider how you can continue to improve your mentoring by reviewing practice at both an individual and school level. After all, two of the assumptions underpinning the process of mentoring are that appropriate feedback is a positive and helpful thing and that you can always continue to develop and improve what you do.

## This evaluation fulfils a lot of different functions

* It provides 'early warning' of things going awry either at the level of individual mentoring partnerships or at the school level.

* It enables you to gauge whether the investment of time and energy you are making is having a worthwhile effect.

* It provides useful 'ammunition' for maintaining, promoting and expanding the use of mentoring in your school.

* It helps you to improve your skills and practices as a mentor.

* It helps you keep a running check on whether the sort of help you are providing as a mentor is what your mentee wants/needs.

* It provides a 'quality assurance' mechanism for the school and some protection for individuals, in case of poor practice or struggling partnerships.

* It sets the right example about feedback, reflective practice and professional development.

So, how exactly should we go about it? Typically, evaluation should take place on a number of different levels.

* **Level 1:** In your individual mentoring partnerships you should adopt a routine of checking in with each other regularly as to how well the mentoring is working and what, if anything, either of you should be doing differently.

* **Level 2:** As a school or college, someone should take responsibility for overseeing the mentoring and seeking feedback on an informal basis.

* **Level 3:** At some point your school needs to undertake a more formal, summative evaluation to assess the impact of mentoring against its original purpose for the school as a whole.

### Today's strategies

1. Oh-ohs and no-nos

2. How you doin'?

3. Can I help?

4. Scores on the doors

# 1. Oh-ohs and no-nos

Underpinning the need for evaluation and monitoring of mentoring is an understanding that such a confidential and potentially intimate series of conversations always has the potential to become problematic or even toxic and damaging. It is not a pleasant thought but, as we saw in the Day 2 chapter, the research evidence from a significant number of mentoring studies in schools confirms that outcomes are not always positive. So, is there a helpful strategy for remembering the key ethical considerations you should be alert to when evaluating your mentoring partnerships?

The following four Cs will hopefully provide a basic framework.

## Confidentiality

One of the potential causes of harm in mentoring relationships is breaches of confidentiality, particularly in small schools where an unguarded comment in the staff room can destroy trust, or even in larger schools or colleges where managers might confuse the confidential content of mentoring sessions with the kind of development information that is recorded and shared.

## Conflict of interest

It may be that your mentoring conversation starts to concern a subject or person in which you have some vested interest. If at any point you feel that you may not be able to remain objective about the topic under discussion, you should declare this and help your mentee find a more appropriate person with whom to explore the issue.

## Competence

As you saw on Day 1, there are boundaries to what is expected of you as a mentor and you should guard against operating outside your areas of competence. This is particularly true of providing counselling or guidance in areas such as marital relationships, stress, depression, or anything else which requires specialist knowledge and skills.

## Co-dependency

If you misjudge your mentee's need for directive help there is a danger that he will become dependent on your wise counsel, instead of developing the resources to better manage his own reflective practice and development. The other side to this coin is that you may get to enjoy being the expert and rely on this to boost your own ego, hence the added danger of co-dependency.

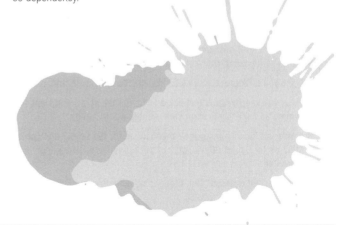

Take a look at the following scenarios and see if you can identify the issue at stake and how you should respond as a responsible mentor.

A.  Your mentee seems to be seeking your advice/approval more and more often.

B.  Your mentee is recounting difficulties he is having with a parent, who happens to be a close personal friend of yours.

C.  Your mentee has complained of stress recently and has been acting strangely and taking more time off ill.

D.  Your mentee is describing how she dealt with a disruptive student and to you this sounds like bullying.

Now take a look at the suggested answers below and see if this is what you thought too.

A.  The potential danger here is one of **dependency**. Remember your aim, as a mentor, is not just to help your mentee to learn, but to improve their ability to manage their own learning. If you are doing this well, your mentee should rely on you less and less, until they reach the point where they no longer need your support. Faced with the situation described here, you should revisit those ground rules you discussed with your mentee and review whether you have perhaps been overly directive in your mentoring approach.

B.  Here we seem to have a classic **conflict of interest**. Can you be as objective and helpful as you need to be, given that you have an emotional stake in the discussion? At the very least, it is important to disclose promptly when you may have a conflict of interest. It may be advisable to suggest that your mentee discusses this dilemma with another one of the school's trained mentors.

C.  You have a duty of care to your mentees, and you want to be helpful, but are you qualified to deal professionally with what may be a medical condition or mental health issue? This is about recognising the limits of your **competence**, and helping your mentee find appropriate sources of help, not playing amateur psychotherapist.

D.  OK, this is maybe a tricky one, not least because I've provided very little information. But the issue at stake is essentially do you 'blow the whistle'? Clearly, you would want to find out more before making this decision, but even at this point you would want to remind your mentee of the limits of **confidentiality**. If this proved to be unacceptable or even illegal behaviour on their part, then keeping it confidential would amount to collusion.

## 2. How you doin'?

Our first level of evaluation is undertaken by the mentor and mentee in each individual partnership. At the very least, you should agree to devote a little time every two or three conversations to checking informally with each other how things are going. Ideally, you should also become adept at spotting more ad hoc opportunities to request feedback from your mentee, particularly if you sense that your questioning or approach is not proving fruitful.

It can help to have some sort of agreed format for this kind of review, so here is one possible strategy.

* **Outcomes:** Start by focusing on what your mentee wants to get out of the mentoring partnership or maybe this specific conversation. Is this clear and agreed between you both? How far is the discussion fulfilling this purpose? What is getting in the way? Does the purpose need to change? Then reverse the roles and talk about what *you* want from the mentoring and how that is going.

* **Process:** Next, review the process of mentoring itself. What are we each doing that is proving helpful? What might we usefully improve? (timing of meetings, preparation, clear objective-setting, amount of challenge/support, balance of talking/listening, etc).

* **Relationship:** Finally (and perhaps most awkwardly!), you need to check how the relationship-building is going. How are we getting on together? Is the process enjoyable? Is anything getting in the way of growing mutual trust and rapport? Yes, this may not be an easy conversation, but that is why it is avoided, often to the mentee's cost.

* **So what?** As with all good mentoring, be sure to conclude with a summary of what, if anything could be improved. Maybe ask the mentee to do this?

### A Spot of Theory

*The European Mentoring and Coaching Council (2009) has a set of competencies for mentors on their website (see Further reading), and includes the following under evaluation:*

* evaluates outcomes with client (and stakeholders if relevant);
* monitors and reflects on the effectiveness of the whole process;
* requests feedback from client on coaching/mentoring;
* receives and accepts feedback appropriately.

Tanya has been mentoring Kurt, an NQT, for two months now and they are having their third meeting. The first two sessions mainly focused on getting to know each other better, and establishing what Kurt wants out of the mentoring. Today they have started looking in earnest at improved lesson planning; one of Kurt's learning goals. Tanya thinks it is time to check how things are going, and has set aside ten minutes at the end of their conversation.

**Tanya:**

" OK Kurt, this is probably the first discussion we've had around a specific learning outcome, so how useful did you find that?

**Kurt:**

" Great, yeah, really helpful…

**Tanya:**

" On a scale of one to ten?

**Kurt:**

" Oh, definitely right up there… an eight I'd say.

**Tanya:**

" That's good to hear. Was there anything we'd set out to achieve today that you don't feel we've covered?

**Kurt:**

" Well, I guess I'm still struggling with what's expected in terms of differentiation. I find it hard sometimes to anticipate how group work is going to pan out timing-wise.

**Tanya:**

" OK, well let's agree now to focus on that next time, shall we? What about the process of mentoring itself? Thinking about the helpfulness of my questions, whether I was understanding you correctly, the structure of the conversation… Anything I could have done differently?

**Kurt:**

" Not really, no. I found it really helpful to follow a logical thought process, and concentrating on one specific lesson worked nicely. You really listened and I felt reassured about what I'm doing right. I suppose you could push me a bit harder maybe on some things. I know I can be a lazy so-and-so sometimes and cut corners…

**Tanya:**

" Right. Noted. Maybe you'll find me a bit more challenging next time! Think we're getting on well enough for that?

**Kurt:**

" Oh dear! I'm going to have to be careful what I wish for aren't I?

**Tanya:**

" Seriously though, how easy are you finding it to confide in me about this stuff? Is there anything I could do to make that easier?

**Kurt:**

" No, I don't think so. I reckon we're getting on fine. But maybe it's time you gave me some feedback. How are things going from your perspective?

## 3. Can I help?

Imagine that you have taken the strategies in this book to heart and suggested to your leadership team that someone needs to take overall responsibility for co-ordinating and monitoring the progress of mentoring in your school. As a result of this, you have been given the job.

So how do you go about informally checking in on the mentors and mentees in a way that will be seen as helpful and discreet as opposed to interfering and nosey? Well, it may be a good idea to give mentoring partnerships sufficient time to have had two or three mentoring conversations (two to three months maybe), and then check in with each person separately and informally to see how things are going and whether they need any more support to ensure the process is helping. This will give you an early warning if anything is going awry and hopefully some useful positive feedback to help maintain commitment to the process, as well as possible topics for further development and support of mentors.

What kind of questions might these informal 'check-ins' include? Well, here are some ideas:

- Have you agreed a clear purpose for
  - each meeting?
  - the partnership as a whole?
- How many meetings have taken place?
- What has been the average length of meetings?
- How often have meetings been changed/cancelled?
- Who is driving the partnership (eg prompting meetings, setting agenda, suggesting changes)?
- How is the mentoring helping you grow as a leader?
- On a scale of 1 to 10 (with 1 being not at all), how much of a rapport do you feel you have with your mentor?
- What, if anything, would you like to improve?

**A Spot of Theory**

*David Clutterbuck, in his book* Everyone Needs a Mentor *(CIPD, 2004), makes the point that evaluation can sometimes feel incompatible with the essential informality of mentoring. Consequently, effective measurement of mentoring needs to be unobtrusive, straightforward and seen as helpful by everyone involved. He suggests four categories of measurement:*

- *relationship processes;*
- *programme processes;*
- *relationship outcomes;*
- *programme outcomes.*

At Bash Street High School the mentoring programme has been in place for about four months or so. Graham, the assistant head with particular responsibility for staff development, is chatting to Sonia, one of his mentors, over a coffee before the school day starts.

**Graham:**

" So, tell me Sonia, how many mentoring sessions have you and Sandhya had so far, and about how much time do you find yourselves spending on each session?

**Sonia:**

" Let's see… it must be three, I think. Yes, because we had a couple in quick succession early on when we were getting to know each other better. I reckon we generally spend anything from an hour to an hour and a half on each session.

**Graham:**

" And how easy has that been? Any cancellations or last-minute changes?

**Sonia:**

" Well, duh! What do you think? To be honest, finding time has been the biggest struggle. So yes, we had to reschedule a couple of times mainly due to last-minute demands on me to be honest.

**Graham:**

" And do you feel like you've established a clear, agreed focus for the mentoring?

**Sonia:**

" Oh yeah. Sandhya poled up at meeting one absolutely clear that she wanted to improve her behaviour management skills.

**Graham:**

" OK that's helpful. So who do you find is driving the partnership, in terms of pinning down meeting times, setting the learning agenda, etc?

**Sonia:**

" Oh, most definitely that's Sandhya. She's been very diligent about preparing herself for discussions and chasing me for meeting times.

**Graham:**

" That's brilliant. It sounds as though you've established a great rapport between you. Is there anything you would change if you could?

**Sonia:**

" Well yes, that's what's so lovely about this. We seem to have struck up a good relationship. From my point of view, I'm fascinated by some of the things that Sandhya does to make the comparative religions curriculum meaningful to her A level students. It's not my subject at all, but it's challenged some of the habits I've perhaps got too comfortable with over the years. I guess if I could change something it would be just growing my own confidence a bit, so the structure and the questioning techniques come a bit more naturally.

*Just need to ask you a couple of questions, and by the way, have you got onto competency 2.3.8 yet?*

---

# 4. Scores on the doors

In addition to informal reviews, the school could benefit from conducting a more detailed evaluation maybe once a year. This will allow you to gather useful feedback from mentors and mentees to help you demonstrate the impact of the mentoring and make improvements to how mentoring operates. This might take the form of a confidential questionnaire to mentors and mentees, and could include questions such as:

- What did you originally want the mentoring to achieve (for you)?
- What were the actual outcomes of the mentoring from your perspective?
- On a scale of 1 to 10 (with 1 being not at all), how satisfied are you with the results of the mentoring?
- How many mentoring meetings have you had?
- How much time in total does this represent?
- What has been the most useful aspect of mentoring for you?
- What have been the biggest hurdles to overcome?
- What further support would be helpful?
- On a scale of 1 to 10 (with 1 being no trust at all and 10 being totally trusting and open), how would you rate the level of trust and openness you achieved?
- What contributed most to this result?

It is this summative evaluation which will also help the school determine the extent to which its institutional objectives have been met (back to the importance of strategy 1!), and whether the cost in time and effort has been worth it.

If you have followed all of the strategies outlined above, you should be in a strong position to act as 'cheerleader' for mentoring in your school. You will have heard lots of positive stories about how it has helped people. You will have heard from mentors about how rewarding they have found the process. You will have some robust data about where mentoring has helped raise school performance. Finally, you will be able to point to continuing improvement and development of mentoring in the future.

All you need to do now is keep feeding it back at every opportunity and provide opportunities for mentors and mentees to celebrate their successes!

## A Spot of Theory

*Writing about implementing mentoring in the FE sector, Susan Wallace and I identified a number of reasons why mentoring programmes can fail.*

- Time demands take their toll on busy colleagues. They need supporting and nurturing to stay committed.
- Poor practice by mentors will stifle creativity and self-reliance, if you don't pick it up and provide further guidance.
- Unclear roles and expectations will soon leave mentors and mentees demotivated and lost.
- Drift resulting from neglect and failure to reinforce people's belief in the benefits of the process will lead to both participants and school leaders losing interest.

At Quantocks College of Further Education, the following piece appeared on the *Quality Improvement at Quantocks* section of the intranet.

### Mentoring update

It's hard to believe that a whole year has passed since we embarked on our mission to make mentoring available to staff as part of their continuing professional development. So what are people saying to us about the impact it has had so far? Our survey says…

* 55% – Received valuable career guidance
* 65% – Got valuable advice on personal development issues
* 54% – Reported greater confidence as a result of mentoring
* 73% – Are satisfied/very satisfied with mentoring
* 81% – Enjoy their mentoring sessions
* 77% – Are happy/very happy with their mentor's skills

Relative to the previous year, staff turnover has decreased, and while this cannot be attributed entirely to mentoring, the anecdotal feedback suggests that it has been a strong factor. Here is just one mentee's experience.

“ *As someone new to teaching, but with a successful previous career running my own business, I was finding that, under pressure, I occasionally lost sight of my own capabilities and what brought me into teaching in the first place. My mentor has been great at helping me maintain my self-confidence and re-connect with what motivates me about this job…*

At an informal 'brown bag' lunch event next month, we aim to get mentors and mentees together to toast a successful first year of the mentoring programme and hear from one brave mentoring partnership about how they tackled their particular learning goals…

*Given the success of our mentoring, we've decided to move from lifelong learning to just getting things right in a week*

**If you only try one thing from this chapter, try this***

Use this to keep a record of what worked well for you and what didn't. Not every strategy will suit every school, or perhaps be practicable. There's a line at the bottom for you to add your own strategy, if it's not already included.

| Strategy | Tried it with... | On...(date) | It worked | It didn't work | Worth trying again? |
|---|---|---|---|---|---|
| 1. Oh-ohs and no-nos | | | | | |
| 2. How you doin'?* | | | | | |
| 3. Can I help? | | | | | |
| 4. Scores on the doors | | | | | |
| Your own strategy? | | | | | |

# Further reading

Clutterbuck, D (2004) *Everyone Needs a Mentor.* 4th ed. London: CIPD.

Connor, M and Pokora, J (2007) *Coaching and Mentoring at Work: Developing Effective Practice*. Maidenhead: Open University Press.

Covey, S R (1989) *The 7 Habits of Highly Effective People*. Latest edition 2013. New York: RosettaBooks.

Cox, E (2005) For Better, For Worse: The Matching Process in Formal Mentoring Schemes. *Mentoring & Tutoring: Partnership in Learning*, 13(3), 403–14.

David, S, Megginson, D and Clutterbuck, D (eds) (2013) *Beyond Goals: Effective Strategies for Coaching and Mentoring*. Farnham: Gower.

De Haan, E (2008) *Relational Coaching: Journeys Towards Mastering One-to-One Learning*. Chichester: John Wiley & Sons Ltd.

Downey, M (2003) *Effective Coaching*. New York: Texere.

Egan, G (2002) *The Skilled Helper*. Pacific Grove, CA: Brooks/Cole.

Ehrich, L C, Hansford, B and Tennent, L (2004) Formal Mentoring Programs in Education and Other Professions: A Review of the Literature. *Educational Administration Quarterly*, 40(4): 518–40.

European Mentoring & Coaching Council. (2009) *Competencies for Mentors*. [online] Available at: https://emccuk.org/wp-content/uploads/2009/10/Competence-Framework-Oct-20092.pdf (accessed 18 November 2016).

Goleman, D (1996) *Emotional Intelligence*. London: Bloomsbury.

Harrison, R (1995) *Collected Papers of Roger Harrison*. New York: McGraw-Hill.

Hobson, A, Ashby, P, Malderez, A and Tomlinson, P (2009) Mentoring Beginning Teachers: What We Know and What We Don't. *Teaching and Teacher Education*, 25: 207–16.

Hope-Hailey, V, Searle, R and Dietz, G, with Abbotson, S, Robinson, V, McCartney, C and Wright, B (2012) *Where Has All the Trust Gone?* London: CIPD. [online] Available at: www.cipd.co.uk/binaries/where-has-all-the-trust-gone_2012-sop.pdf (accessed 18 November 2016).

Klasen, N and Clutterbuck, D (2002) *Implementing Mentoring Schemes: A Practical Guide to Successful Programs*. Oxford: Butterworth Heinemann.

Kline, N (2009) *More Time to Think*. Pool-in-Wharfedale: Fisher King Publishing.

Kolb, D (1984) *Experiential Learning: Experience as the Source of Learning and Development*. Englewood Cliffs, NJ: Prentice Hall.

McAdams, D P (1993) *The Stories We Live By: Personal Myths and the Making of the Self*. Guilford Press.

Megginson, D and Clutterbuck, D (2005) *Techniques for Coaching and Mentoring*. Oxford: Butterworth Heinemann.

Megginson, D and Clutterbuck, D (2009) *Further Techniques for Coaching and Mentoring*. Oxford: Butterworth Heinemann.

Megginson, D, Clutterbuck, D, Garvey, B, Stokes, P and Garrett-Harris, R (2006) *Mentoring in Action: A Practical Guide*. 2nd ed. London: Kogan Page.

Offman, D (2001) *Inspiration and Quality in Organisations*. 12th ed. Utrecht, Antwerpen: Kosmos-Z&K.

Rogers, C (1951) *Client-centred Therapy*. Boston: Houghton Mifflin.

Rogers, J (2001) *Adults Learning*. 4th ed. Buckingham: Open University Press.

Rogers, J (2004) *Coaching Skills*. Buckingham: Open University Press.

Scandura, T (1998) Dysfunctional Mentoring Relationships and Outcomes. *Journal of Management*, 24(3): 449–67.

Stokes, P (2003) Exploring the Relationship between Mentoring and Counselling. *British Journal of Guidance & Counselling*, 31(1).

Teaching Schools Council (2016) *National Standards for School-based Initial Teacher Training (ITT) Mentors*. [online] Available at: www.gov.uk/government/uploads/system/uploads/attachment_data/file/536891/Mentor_standards_report_Final.pdf (accessed).

Wallace, S and Gravells, J (2007) *Mentoring*. Exeter: Learning Matters.

Wilkins, P (2000) Unconditional Positive Regard Reconsidered. *British Journal of Guidance & Counselling*, 28(1): 23–36.

**CRITICAL** PUBLISHING

Register with Critical Publishing to:

* be the first to know about forthcoming titles;

* find out more about our new Getting it Right in a Week series;

* sign up for our regular newsletter for special offers, discount codes and more.

Visit our website at:

www.criticalpublishing.com

Notes